The advice and strategies found within may not be suitable for every situation. This work is sold with the understanding that neither the author nor the publisher are held responsible for the results accrued from the advice in this book.

Can we guarantee that the methods in this book will catch carp every session? Nope, this is fishing, remember. However, we can guarantee that the techniques in this book will catch carp.

Guaranteed Carp:

The Comprehensive Carp Fishing Guide

Table of Contents

Introduction

Introduction to Carp Fishing

Carp fishing has grown as a massively popular sport globally, especially in the UK and some parts of Europe where Carp are seen as high-class sport fish. Carp grow to ridiculous sizes, and their powerful tails and heavy bodies make for a great fight; it's no surprise this sport has become so popular. In the UK, millions of anglers target carp and other coarse fish, with this number growing significantly every year as we progress into a new decade.

Carp fishing, in the most basic terms possible, is going out to catch the carp species using a rod, reel and various other fishing tackle. Carp fishing has its specific fishing methods that are rarely used for other types of fishing. As this fish has particulate feeding habits and is known for being hard to catch, new fishing methods have been developed over the year by experienced carp anglers.

Nowadays, carp fishing is huge across the UK and Europe with millions of anglers devoting time to fishing for carp species. In this book, you're going to find vast amounts of information that will help to brush up your carp fishing knowledge and get you into catching some more carp. You'll find the following in this book so make sure you keep reading:

- Carp and Coarse Fish descriptions and distinctive features.
- Carp behaviours and how to use them to your advantage.
- How to select the best carp fishing tackle for your approach.
- How to use "watercraft" to your advantage.
- The best baits to use and why.
- The seven most effective carp rigs and the best situations to use each.
- How to protect your catch once it is on the banks.

History of Carp Fishing

Carp are fish from the large "Cyprinidae" family that is native to Europe and Asia. Nowadays, carp can be found across nearly every continent on the planet. It is thought that carp were first introduced into the UK by the 15th century by monks. These monks domesticated the wild fish from mainland Europe and kept them in ponds on abbey grounds to provide food. The monks very closely controlled access to the fish in these abbey ponds, so these fish's soft white meat was not available to the masses. Back in these times, carp meat was seen as an extremely high-value food.

Selective breeding allowed for these relatively small wild fish to begin growing to then unprecedented sizes. This selective breeding began the transition into breeding the massive fish we have swimming in our waters today. Over these initial years of Carp in the UK, escapees and transfers into rivers and lakes began spreading Carp in UK waters. Due to carp yielding hundreds of thousands of eggs per spawn, the "wilder" population began to proliferate.

As carp are bottom feeders and often feed on vegetation, these fish may have saved some native species such as Rudd and Tench. The hundreds of thousands of eggs expelled into the waters during the carp spawn also provide a food source for native fish.

History of Carp Fishing

The angling side of carp in the UK started in the late years of the 19th century when new variations of these fish got imported from Europe. This importation began with the importation of the mirror carp from Holland and Germany. Thomas Ford, who owned "Manor Fisheries" was the first man to kick start carp angling in the UK. Imported fish were stocked in his pond and were often over 10lbs, which dwarfed the native fish such as the perch and roach that anglers commonly caught.

Due to their sheer size and reputation for being hard to catch, the carp fishing craze started. Anglers came from far and wide to try to catch some of these fish. Donald Leany was the next big name to start importing carp into the UK. He imported hundreds of thousands of these fish which were used to stock some of the most famous fisheries in the UK today. The selective breeding from breeders across Europe and the UK is why carp are massively different in sizes and shapes today.

Originally fish from Holland could grow to unimaginable sizes through sustained bone growth for longer than usual. On the other hand, fish imported from Italy would reach impressive weights but not grow as long as the Dutch fish. This meant that these large fish were nearly as deep as they were long. As the carp angling buzz spread across the UK and fisheries within the country started to breed these fish, plenty of fisheries began to open up across the country.

Have you ever looked at your net filled with your latest catch and thought, what type of carp even is that? We certainly did in the beginning. For beginner carp anglers differentiating between each species and sub-species can be somewhat confusing as there are so many types of carp. Still, it's not that difficult at all.

Each has its own distinct features and, with a bit of knowledge, can be easily identified; that is what you will find in this section. We can almost guarantee you'll know exactly what carp you've caught, maybe even before it hits the net after reading this section of the book.

We all know the typical carp species popular amongst fishermen, such as the common, mirror, grass, crucian, koi, and leather carp in the UK. These will be discussed in the chapter's first half. The second part is aimed a little differently, with the hopes of showing you some other coarse species that you will be likely to come across when targetting carp.

Common Carp

Background

Well, where do we start? The common carp is occasionally referred to as the "European Carp" or "Cyprinus carpio". Considering this carp has the word "common" in its name, you would assume that you will have more chance of catching this species at commercial fisheries. Surprisingly, this is not the case.

Fisheries will often stock a larger quantity of "mirror carp" so hooking into a massive common is an exhilarating experience.

The common carp is native to Europe and Asia but is introduced into nearly every part of the world. It was even farmed for food dating back to as far as Roman times. Nowadays, in the UK, this is not the case as carp are primarily stocked for the satisfaction of anglers. "Native" common Carp are currently marked as "vulnerable" to extinction by the International Union for Conservation of Nature. This is quite surprising considering the abundance of carp in many lakes and rivers worldwide, but most of these fish are classed as "domesticated." They have been bred for angling or introduced to control aquatic plants and pest organism.

Carp are classified as an invasive species and feature in the list of the top 100 invasive species. They are seen as pests in many areas due to their ability to out-compete native fish species.

Distinctive Features

So how do you know if you've caught a common carp? Well, it's straightforward. Common Carp are covered with regular scales ranging from grey to bronze in colour. Common Carp have four barbels and a large elongated dorsal fin which can be seen in the picture above. "Domestic" carp grow a lot larger than native carp and are much larger with deeper bodies. These carp have giant mouths, perfect for gulping down large boilies.

Mirror Carp

Types of Carp

Background

Mirror carp are a sub species of the common carp and was the first mutation of common carp. Biologically mirror carp are almost identical to its predecessor, the common carp. The lack of scales found on the mirror carp is commonly thought to be from breeding of monks to make the fish easier to consume as fewer scales must be removed before serving.

Mirror carp are thought to have been introduced into Britain in the 15th century as a food source. Nowadays, mirror carp are mainly bred and introduced into commercial fisheries for us anglers. Like the common carp they put up an extremely good fight and grow to unreal sizes in the right environments.

As well as breeding for fewer scales mirror carp were also bred to grow to greater sizes than commons which can be clearly shown with the most recent world record. The reason for this is that commons take a lot of energy growing scales covering their full body whereas mirror put this energy to growing in overall size rapidly.

The world record mirror carp stands at an unbelievable 108lbs (November 2018) and was caught in Hungary at Euro Aqua fishery.

Distinctive Features

Mirror carp are visually different from common carp as they have irregular and patchy scales shown in the picture above. All mirror carps scale patterns are different, giving them a sense of character. Mirror carp tend to have a rounder appearance than common carp. Mirror carp also have giant mouths like the commons and two barbells at each side of their mouths.

Grass Carp

Background

The grass carp or "Ctenopharyngodon Idella" is another species of carp and native to China. The grass carp was introduced into many countries worldwide, including Europe and the United States, for aquatic weed control. They were first introduced in the UK on the Lancaster canal as an experiment into weed control conducted by British Waterways and the University of Liverpool.

Grass carp reproduce in water temperatures over 20 degrees Celsius, so in the UK, they cannot reproduce naturally. This allows their population to be carefully controlled by the Environmental agency, unlike commons and mirrors. It was thought that grass carp would take little interest in commercial fishing baits, but this was soon discarded as more and more and more grass carp were caught by anglers. Grass carp grow rapidly most likely because they eat up to three times their body weight each day!

Distinctive Features

Grass carp are quite dark and range from yellowish to brown. Grass carp are longer and slimmer and have "torpedo like" body shape and lack barbels beside their mouths. The anal fin is located closer to the tail. Grass carp have sale patterns similar to commons. As you can see from the picture grass carps dorsal fins are smaller and not as long as commons or mirrors which helps to easily identify them. They have low flat heads, and their mouths are a lot smaller than mirrors and commons.

Leather Carp

Background

The leather carp is another subspecies of the common carp and is thought to be a mirror carp with no scales, but this is not the case with leather carp having some distinct genetic differences from mirrors. Leather carp have fewer red blood cells than mirrors or commons, which stunts their growth. Due to this, hooking into an oversized leather is an achievement, and they are known to put up an excellent fight.

Distinctive Features

Leather carp have near enough no scales apart from an occasional row across the dorsal line and the base of the tale. A "perfect" leather carp has no scales at all. Their skin looks almost like leather hence the name; from this they can be easily identified. Leather carp's colour can range from dark green to dark bronze. The anal fin often has fewer rays than commons and mirrors, and the dorsal fin is often imperfect.

Crucian Carp

Background

The Crucian Carp is another member of the carp family and is the smallest out of them all. It shows up widely across Europe and can even be found as far north as the Arctic Circle in Scandinavian countries. They can survive in conditions that many other fish cannot deal with, including the smallest of weedy, muddy pools to icy waters. Catching a sizeable crucian carp can be rather challenging as they are the most delicate feeders from the carp family.

Even a 2lb crucian is considered a great catch which puts into perspective how small these fish are compared to all other carp species discussed in this book. Instead of gulping in baits, crucian carp tend to nudge the bait and suck very gently to check for our hooks. This can become highly frustrating to carp anglers targeting these fish. But still, if you intend to target these fish, they can usually be found near drop-offs into deep water.

Distinctive Features

As stated, crucian carp is the smallest of the carp family and rarely grows over 6 lbs. Crucian carp are usually golden or bronze looking and darken with age. They have yellow or orangeish fins. Crucian carp are quite tall fish as they mature. Crucian carp have no barbells.

Koi Carp

Background

The Koi carp was initially bred in Japan in the 1820s in the town of Ojiya for its bright colours. The word Koi, therefore, comes from Japan and simply translates to "carp". Apart from select areas in Japan, the Koi carp were never seen by the outside world until 1914, after they were displayed at a public exhibition in Tokyo.

After this, the Koi carp took off and many new variations were bred. Keeping Koi carp as a hobby spread quickly across the world and they were mostly kept as ornamental fish. There is now thought to be more than 22 varieties of Koi, with new variations being actively developed. Each variety has certain distinct colours, patterns, and specific scaling.

Koi have been released into near enough every continent except Antarctica, but they quickly revert to the colouration of common carp in only a few generations. Keeping Koi in a pond puts them at a severe disadvantage against predators.

Due their prominent colouration, predators, including herons, badgers, otters, foxes and even cats, can be capable of emptying an entire pond of your hobby fish if measures aren't taken to avoid this.

Well-designed ponds have areas too deep for Herons to stand, overhangs so mammals can't reach in, and trees above the ponds so any birds flying past can't spot their next meal in the water.

Distinctive Features

Koi carp are the easiest to identify due to their obscure and bright colour patterns. Koi Carp come in many colours that include white, black, red, orange, yellow, blue, and cream in all different patterns. The colours are near enough limitless.

Koi Carp are incredibly similar to goldfish in shape, but they grow much larger and have two barbels that goldfish do not.

F1 Carp

Background

The F1 Carp is a relatively new species to the UK but is now commonly one of the most stocked. The F1 Carp is a hybrid between common and crucian carp so is smaller than commons or mirrors. This crossbreeding occurs naturally in the wild but these fish are widely bred for stocking commercial fishing waters.

F1 Carp feed all year round so grow rapidly. This is one of the reasons why this new species of carp is in such high demand. Although F1 grow quickly they don't grow to the massive sizes of other carp species. They usually grow to around under 5lbs with some exceptions.

Distinctive Features

F1 Carp can be hard to identify as they look a lot like a smaller common. A way to determine if you have caught an F1 carp is to look at their barbells. F1 carp only have two smaller barbells compared to common carps four barbel

When fishing for carp in the UK or Europe it is extremely common to come across other fish species that enjoy your bait just as much as members of the carp family. Below you'll find a list of the most common course species you'll come across.

Bream

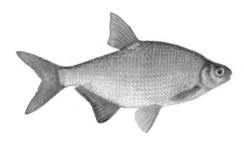

Background

If you've caught a slim, slimy fish, it's probably a bream. Typically found in still waters, bream is a common species of coarse fish. It typically feeds near the bottom and is termed as a 'bottom-feeder' just like carp. Bream are omnivores that feed on almost anything they can find — small crustaceans, fish, algae, molluscs, etc. They're all fair game for bream! But how can you tell when you've caught a bream? Let's see.

Distinctive Features

So, how can you positively identify bream? They have translucent, silver-grey scales. These silver-grey fish turn slightly bronze the older that bream grow. They are also deep-bodied, which means their bodies are flattened from the sides but have a tall physique.

They grow to maximum lengths ranging from 1-2 feet while weighing anywhere from 5-8 lb. Anglers use the pectoral fin sometimes to identify bream. This technique depends on the pectoral fins colour as it takes on a reddish hue as the bream grows into an adult.

Barbel

Background

Some species are easy to remember because their names tell you their most important feature. Barbels are known for the pairs of barbels extending from the sides of their mouth. These barbels help them to judge food based on smell and touch. They also grow rapidly and are powerful. Barbel live in rivers and scavenge for food such as crustaceans, snails, molluscs, etc., near the riverbed

Distinctive Features

Barbel has a typical bottom-feeder mouth. Which mouth is that you wonder? Bottom-feeders typically have mouths that point downwards, which helps them scavenge food more efficiently at the bottom of the water.

They also have pairs of two fleshy barbels on each side of their mouth. These barbels are what give this fish its name. Sizes can widely vary, with some barbel growing to 1.5 inches and others growing to over 21lbs in the UK. Barbel are light green to light brown.

Gudgeon

Background

Gudgeon are quite possibly the most uncomplicated fish among all the coarse fish. Gudgeon are small fish that predator fish anglers may use as bait. They are members of the carp family. One can usually find them in fast-flowing waters such as rivers, etc. They tend to feed on smaller animals or fish. Gudgeon, much like other members of the carp family, are bottom feeders.

Distinctive Features

Gudgeon have elongated bodies and downward protruding mouths. They are grey-green. There is a fleshy barbel on each side of the gudgeon's mouth. They are relatively small and do not grow beyond the length of 8 inches. Gudgeon also have small spots lining the sides of their body.

Chub

Background

Another angler favourite is the chub. The common chub is also sometimes referred to as the European chub. These chub typically prey on other small animals, insects, etc. They usually do not grow beyond the length of 2 feet.

They are a popular species of coarse fish. Angler's love catching chub because they fight hard. You can often find chub in shaded, secluded spots such as the spots with branches hanging over them, just like carp.

Distinctive Features

Chub have largish scales that are green and brown. A contrasting black colour streaks its edges. In comparison, chub have very pale bellies. They have rounded bodies, and their snouts are blunt.

Dace

Background

These fish are huge fans of eating whatever comes their way. Dace are small fish that anglers sometimes confuse with chub. Anglers typically find them near the surface of the water. Anglers can discover dace in brackish waters as well as rivers and streams. Dace are voracious feeders and will eat almost anything.

Most anglers catch dace by using maggots and bread as bait. Many anglers also use dace as baitfish owing to their small size. Some parts of the world eat dace, but it is mainly considered an inedible coarse fish in the UK and its surroundings.

Distinctive Features

Dace are silvery-blue in colour and have inferior mouths. Their upper jaw is much longer than their lower jaw. They also have a forked tail. Dace have large, silver scales that cover their entire body. Their bodies are slender, and they are set apart by their bright yellow eyes. Their bellies are lighter in colour than the rest of their bodies.

Perch

Background

Perch are typically fresh-water fish with two common types. These types are the common perch and the yellow perch but these are only commonly found outside the UK. One commonly finds them near river or lake banks, and anglers catch them by using maggots or even spinners as bait.

Anglers can usually catch them in still, or slow-moving waters. Unlike other common coarse fish species, perch are not omnivores. Instead, they feed exclusively on smaller fish and larvae. White perch are considered as coarse fish; some parts of the world also eat them. Anglers like them because they are active fighters when caught.

Distinctive Features

Common perch are typically greenish-brown in colour. Their most striking feature is the set of dark, vertical lines that one can see across their body. They have round bodies and usually grow to a weight of 6.6 lb or so (very uncommon). Their dorsal fins are sharp and pointy.

Roach

Background

Roach is similar in shape to carp. They are not very big, and anglers usually catch them as a sport. They are a robust species of fish that can survive in extremely harsh conditions as well. Their population in local rivers and lakes is large. Roach are omnivores that eat various food such as plants or algae and small invertebrate animals and maggots, etc.

Distinctive Features

Roach have a metallic silver-blue colour. Their fins contrast from the rest of the silver body by being red-brown. Roach, like most other coarse fish, have a pale belly. They also have red eyes and are relatively small in size. Their back is darker in colour as compared to the rest of their body. Young roach are more slender. You can identify roach by an unmistakable red mark over their pupil.

Rudd

Background

It's time to concentrate because many people confuse rudd with roach. Rudd are more colourful than other coarse fish. However, roach can easily be differentiated from rudd by the red marks in their eyes. They are usually present in slow-moving waters with a lot of vegetation. Rudd are omnivores, usually eating any plants, insects, etc. However, older ones tend to have more herbivore eating patterns.

Like carp, people also consider rudd to be destructive species. This status is because they tend to dirty any water they inhabit, destroy all vegetation in that particular part of the water and compete with other smaller fish species for food.

Distinctive Features

Their fins are orange in colour, while the rest of their body is present in varying shades of silver and orange. They are deep-bodied and built stoutly. They have shiny, reflective scales that are silver in colour. They usually do not grow beyond 14-15 inches. Rudd have mouths that point upwards, as this allows them to feed more quickly near the surface. They also look greenish-yellow at times.

Tench

Background

Tench are, interestingly, also called 'the doctor fish.' Anglers usually find them in shallow waters that have a lot of vegetation in them. Tench also have fleshy barbels extending from the sides of its mouth. They use these barbels to judge and find food, just like carp.

They are referred to as doctor fish because an old wives' tale describes them as the fish that other sick fish rubbed against to get healthy again. They are very tough and can withstand various conditions such as low oxygen concentration in the water, muddy waters, and a high vegetation level.

Distinctive Features

Tench are carp-like in body shape. They have a light green colour that becomes golden towards their underside. Tench also have barbels on each side of their mouth. However, these barbels are smaller than the typical barbels that you see in coarse fish. Tench have tiny scales and a broad, square tail. They have an extremely slimy exterior, which makes them highly slippery upon catching. They also have small, reddish eyes.

Ide

Background

Ide is another coarse fish that looks like carp. They are considered edible, and anglers catch them as a sport. They typically reside in large bodies of water. A lot of people confuse ide with chub. However, a closer look can help anglers differentiate between the two.

Ide are usually omnivores, but older ide primarily feeds on other, smaller fish. Anglers also love to catch ide for their habit of fighting hard when caught.

Distinctive Features

Ide has stout bodies that are silvery in colour. They are deep-bodied and have yellow eyes. They usually grow to around 10-12 inches in length. Ide also possesses pharyngeal teeth. Although most id weigh anywhere between 1 or 2 kg, some anglers have caught ide weighing almost 5kg.

Carp Behaviours

Carp Behaviours

Before getting deep into carp angling, we will focus more on carp behaviours in this chapter. If you don't know their behaviours, how are you going to catch them?

By taking a step away from carp fishing techniques to read more about how they feed, swim, and act, you gain vital knowledge that will be used for your fishing. In this chapter we are going to cover:

- A discussion if carp meet the requirements of a bottom feeder and how this impacts the fishing approach to catch these fish.
- Why carp jump out of the water and how you can use these visuals signs to target fish to catch.
- How carp feed under the waters surface to give you an idea of how these fish will react to your baits in the water.

Are Carp Bottom Feeders?

So, as a starting point, we'll cover what a bottom feeder is and what characteristics a fish must have to be classed as one, and of course, how this relates to carp. According to the Google dictionary, a bottom feeder is;

> ***"any marine creature that lives on the seabed and feeds by scavenging"***

Sound like Carp? Not too far away, we'd say.

Although this definition seems to focus on sea-dwelling creatures, their fresh-water equivalents can also be classed as bottom feeders as they feed on the lakebed. As bottom feeders spend a lot of time on the lake or seabed, they have flat undersides or "flat ventral regions". This allows the fish to easily rest their bodies on the bottom when scavenging for food.

Another common feature of bottom feeders is the "inferior mouth ". An inferior mouth is another way of saying the fish has a downturned mouth that will point towards the lakebed. It makes sense for bottom-feeding fish to swim horizontally and sift through the silt below with a downturned mouth.

Going by this definition, it would seem that; Yes, carp fit within the bottom-feeding category but let's look into why this is the case and why some people might not believe they are purely bottom feeders. As a lot of you will already know, carp spend a lot of time feeding on the bottom and scavenging for natural food such as insects, crustaceans, worms, plant matter and anything that looks edible enough.

As far as having a "flat ventral region though" this might not be 100% true for carp. This mainly refers to fish with various rays and even hammerhead sharks that are extremely flat on the bottom to consistently move across the flat bottom. For carp, this is not the case but does this make them a non-bottom feeder? Nope, not at all.

They also have an apparent inferior downturned mouth that is perfect for sifting through the silt on the lake's bottom and inhaling anything edible they find on their hunt. Although carp are well-known as bottom feeders, this is not the only place they feed, and they probably only feed on the bottom for 40-50% of the time.

Carp feed in nearly all sections of the water column and are even known to feed directly on the surface. It is no wonder that some people would not class carp as bottom feeders when in fact, they are.

Where else do Carp Feed?

Carp generally feed throughout the water column from the bottom, mid-water and even the surface in certain conditions. Generally, carp will be feeding will depend on the type of year, weather conditions and even what body of water you're fishing. You'll need to hold on to this thought, and we'll discuss this further in "Chapter 4 Watercraft".

Why do Carp Jump?

Spotting carp jumping out of the water gets the adrenaline pumping for us carp anglers. Whether it's a 5lb carp or a 30lb brute, watching carp jump and swirl on the surface guarantees there are carp in the area for catching.

But why do carp jump out of the water? Unfortunately, the answer isn't as simple as you'd think. There are many reasons why carp leap from the water; some of these reasons might even indicate feeding patterns. You could hook yourself into some nice fish with a bit of knowledge on why these fish tend to jump.

Anatomical Reason

The main reason carp can be seen leaping straight of the water is anatomical and most likely won't give any tell-tale signs of feeding patterns, so purely quite dull if you ask us. But anyway, you are here to find out why carp jump out of the water, so we'll tell you just that.

Carp, like all fish, have swim bladders. These swim bladders control buoyancy in the water and, therefore, the depth at which the carp swims. The swim bladder is linked to the oesophagus, and by varying the air within their swim bladder, the fish can rise or drop in the water column.

Why do Carp Jump?

When carp jump from the water, air is forced in or out of the swim bladder through the oesophagus, allowing carp to change depths. On shallower water, the chances of seeing fish jump are reduced quite significantly as not much pressure is built up with depth changes. However, in deeper water, you will tend to see more activity of carp leaping.

Don't get me wrong; carp will not always jump to change swimming depths as they could do this through natural processes. If carp leapt from the water every time they changed depth carp fishing would be even more of an interesting experience.

In lakes where carp travel from depths to the surface, pressure increases on their swim bladder, so jumping and forcing air from their swim bladder neutralises this pressure so the carp can swim properly in the upper layers of the water.

Cleaning Method

Another reason that seems to hold its own is that carp leap out of the water as a method of cleaning out debris from their gills. As you all now know, carp are mainly bottom feeders and suck up food from the waterbed. Of course, as the carp suck in food particles, dirt and debris can also be taken in and build up in their gills.

So why not clean out this debris with a leap out of the water? When the carp hit the surface, water rushes through their gills, washing out any built-up silt or mud.

Carp tend to find themselves bothered by parasites, so it is commonly thought that carp jump from the water to rouse themselves from these parasites. The force of the carp hitting the water is a method of scrubbing parasites from their bodies.

Types of Jumping

Now onto the fun part. We're sure you would like to find out what these jumps mean relative to fishing. The bottom line is, there is no guaranteed answer, but by analysing patterns in carp fishing, it is thought there are four ways that carp will jump, which are considered to show slightly different signs;

Crashing

Crashing is where the carp leap right out of the water and, unsurprisingly, come crashing down on the surface, causing a large splash. The commonly thought reason for carp doing this is as a cleaning method. A large splash can be enough to rid them of tricky parasites.

If the carp are jumping over silty parts of the venue, this could indicate the carp are feeding and jumping to clear their gills of silt before going back down to feed some more. If this is the case, it's recommended to get a bait in this area ASAP as chances are there are more than one carp feeding.

Try casting past the area and reeling back as to not spook the carp out of their feeding. If the carp are crashing from areas that are not thought to be silty, they are most likely just trying to rid themselves of parasites, so casting bait to them will most likely not give you any more chance of catching them.

Head and shouldering

Head and shouldering is where, also unsurprisingly, the carp leave the water until their head and shoulders are visible on the surface with slightly less of a splash. This is also thought to indicate feeding carp as they leave the water to rid their gills of any silt and mud build-ups.

If you see this, it'd be wise to cast a bait to this area as once again; there's a chance there will be more than one carp feeding.

Rolling

Rolling is where the carp "roll" on the surface. You are more likely to see this on large bodies of water as the carp group up and move to new parts of the water. This won't necessarily indicate feeding and the chance to catch these carp, but you can watch where these carp are heading.

If you can get a few rods into where these carp are heading to feed, you could be in with a chance of having an action-packed session. If the carp are rolling and splashing in the shallows in large numbers, then the chances are the carp are spawning. Unfortunately, if this is the case, your chances of catching these fish is near enough zero.

Head poking

As you can imagine, this is where the carp poke their heads from the water. This is almost always thought to be a sign of carp feeding as they come to the surface to rid their gills of silt before plunging back to eat some more.

If you spot this on the water, get a bait in there as soon as possible and your chances of catching can be greatly increased. Carp are also known to stick with habits so remember this area of the water for your next sessions to give yourself an extra edge over the fish. Or are they just checking what peg we are on to try to avoid us?

Now you should be more than familiar with why carp tend to jump; you can put this into practice to spot signs of carp on the water. There will be more on reading these signs of carp further through the book.

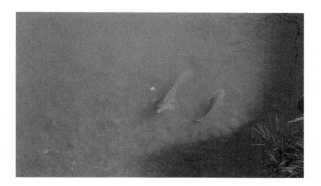

Many carp anglers that frequent the banks of your local carp fishing venues like to believe they know how to catch carp, and in a lot of cases, this will be the case. However, one thing that many anglers lack knowledge of is how carp behave beneath the surface. By learning these carp habits and behaviours, you can significantly increase your catch rates.

We've already covered where carp feed in the water column, but in this section, we will focus on how carp feed to provide you with all the knowledge you'll need on how carp feed below the surface with a look at anatomical and movement factors. This knowledge should aid you in planning approaches to your subsequent fishing sessions to hopefully get a good few more fish on the banks.

How Carp Feed

To get to the bottom of how carp feed, there will be references to various scientific studies that have been carried out to gain more significant insights into the feeding patterns of carp. These studies get rather technical rather quickly, but we'll try to keep it as easy to understand as possible so you can work out how these feeding behaviours relate to your carp fishing.

Feeding Mechanisms in Carp

To fully get to grips with how carp feed, the first study we will discuss is "Feeding Mechanisms in Carp ". This study was conducted to determine how carp filter food to consume only food particles and expel inorganic particles.

The study was carried out with a focus on carp during "benthic" feeding. This may sound confusing, but it just means when carp are feeding on the bottom. Due to carp being bottom feeders, a lot of their feeding time will be "benthic".

This study aimed to find out how carp can segregate between the edible food resting on the lake's bottom and the inedible food stuffs such as gravel, small stones and other debris at the bottom of the lake. This is highly relevant to us anglers as this sheds light on how the fish are consuming the bottom baits in the swim you are fishing which will give you an idea of how particle baits such as groundbait (more on this bait later) are ingested.

The study investigates two ways it is thought that carp consume and sort food sources from non-food sources when bottom feeding. These two hypotheses are as follows;

- "when engulfing food mixed with inorganic particles during benthic feeding, cyprinid fish use protrusions of tissue from the palatal organ to retain the food particles while the inorganic particles are expelled from the opercular slits."
- "In crossflow filtration, the particle suspension is pumped parallel to the filter surface as filtrate exits through the filter pores, causing the suspension to become more concentrated as it travels downstream along the filter."

Carp Feeding

- "We used high-speed video endoscopy to determine whether carp *Cyprinus carpio* use crossflow filtration and/or palatal protrusions during benthic feeding"

I'm sure you now know what I mean by these studies getting technical rather quickly but don't worry we'll break this down into basic terms.

The first thing the study looks at is if feeding carp use lumps of tissue at the back of the mouth (buccopharyngeal cavity) to keep the edible particles and then expel the non-edible particles through the "opercular slits" or part of the gills in more basic terms.

The next thing that is looked at is if carp use crossflow filtration to separate these edible particles. This is sieving particles through "filters" in the fish's mouth that can determine and retain edible substances and expel inedible substances through mainly taste.

It was found that carp when feeding on small particles, don't seem to use the lumps of tissues to keep edible parts. However, when larger food stuffs were fed, these bumps were used to retain these and then the larger inedible debris was spat out from the mouth.

When food particles with lower density than the inorganic materials were sucked into the mouths of the carp, cross-flow filtration allowed for large numbers of less dense food particles to be separated rapidly from large numbers of inedible substances.

This study helps to show precisely how carp consume different types of feed, from groundbaits and particle baits on the bottom to more significant food substances such as micro pellets.

Food Handling in Carp

The subsequent study that helps to shed light on how carp feed and their behaviours under the water is the study of "Food Handling in Carp ".

This study focused more on carp behaviours and not so much on the anatomical areas of carp feeding.

This section will help show you exactly how the carp interact with food stuffs such as large boilies and pellets to show you why carp might sometimes investigate your bait without getting hooked.

Light and x-ray cinematography was used to build a picture of the external and internal process of carp consuming various food types.

Ten patterns of head movements were recorded with distinct feeding actions. These twelve feeding patterns were;

- Particulate feeding
- Gulping for intake
- Rinsing
- Repositioning
- Selective retention
- Gathering from branchial sieve
- Transport
- Loading of teeth
- Crushing
- Grinding
- Deglutition

Carp Feeding

The study suggests that carp have a high level of energy at dusk and night but are readily trained to feed at any time of the day, but if you want to improve your chances get out on the bank at these times.

The twelve feeding steps follow a sequence like the one below.

1. Carp use their olfactory system to sense salt, flavours and particles in the water that bring them in from the surrounding areas to your bait, but we'll discuss this a little further later on.
2. Once the carp has found your bait they position their larger mouth over the bait and suck rapidly, propelling the bait into their mouth where it is fixed between the upper and lower jaw for under a second.
3. The fish rapidly pumps water over the bait and washes off any silt or inedible matter and then tastes the bait to investigate if it's worth swallowing or not.
4. This takes around two seconds. If the carp likes what it tastes, the bait will be repositioned to the front of the mouth by drawing water through the gills with its mouth closed. In this position the bait will be further washed by pumping water through the mouth. This step is quite often missed out if the bait is "clean" after the first rinse. If it's not too keen on the bait it will spit the bait back out and move on.
5. If the carp has chosen to consume the food item, it will be slowly positioned to the back of the throat, where the teeth are found.
6. The fish will then wait a few seconds before the "chewing" begins.
7. The chewing lasts for around a few seconds, and the fish's mouth remains open during the process.
8. The food is then swallowed to complete the feeding process.

By knowing this feeding sequence, your rigs and bait setup can start to make a little more sense.

When carp suck in your bait, they spend a few seconds tasting. If you have hooked your bait straight onto a hook, you run the risk of the carp spitting the bait because of the strange object in the food.

Therefore, hair rigs come into play. By leaving your bait directly off the hook, you reduce the risk of the carp sensing anything wrong with the bait and moving to the next stage where your hook will be sucked fully into the carp's mouth.

How do Carp Find Food

It's all excellent knowing how carp will consume your bait once they have found it, but how exactly do they find your bait in the first place? You'll find out in this section. Carp are great foragers and use various methods for scouring for food in every layer of water. Just because carp are bottom feeders, they don't necessarily always feed on the bottom.

Carp use their sense of smell, eyesight and even an olfactory system that lets them sense any dissolved foodstuff in the water.

The carp use the following method for sourcing food;

- **Barbels** – Two barbels protrude from the side of the carp's mouth, with two smaller barbels above the mouth. These are not just for show and are used to detect food on the bottom of the body of water directly under its mouth where it can't quite see. These barbels also have taste buds that quickly detect if the item they are touching is edible or not.
- **Mouth** – Carp have an excellent sense of taste as their mouths have chemical sensitive cells that define if a food substance is edible or not. Carp expel around 97% of what they take into their mouth for tasting.
- **Pectoral and Pelvic Fins** – The carp's fins are lined by taste buds that further aid in finding food sources close to the fish.
- **Eyes** – These fish have excellent vision with two eyes on either side of the head. This vision is used to not only look for predators, anglers on the banks included; they also use them for sourcing food. This is why brightly coloured baits seem to work well as the carp's attention is drawn to them.
- **Olfactory System** – The olfactory system allows the fish to sense dissolved substances in the water such as salts, sugars and proteins in baits that help bring carp in from the surrounding area to your baits.

These reports and studies are great at taking a greater look into how carp feed even though they are somewhat technical at some points.

We have tried to decipher the technical jargon and provide you with easy-to-understand information to thoroughly learn the carp feeding process.

By knowing this added information, you should be able to add an extra edge to your fishing, and it will even give you some more information to spread around your fishing partners.

Carp Fishing Tackle

Carp Fishing Tackle

Carp fishing is one of those things that requires the perfect mixture of technique, equipment, and experience for it all to come together nicely. Whether you're an experienced angler doing a little night-time reading or a beginner leafing through the pages of this book for some helpful tips, remember the most important thing: *The tackle you use is a critical aspect of your carp fishing experience.*

Whether it is an unsuitable rod or rig for the fishing you're doing, you'll soon learn that stocking up on a suitable tackle is the first key to succeeding at carp fishing. Although this doesn't need to get overly expensive. If you're struggling with casting well, there's a chance that you don't have the best rod for the situation. In this section, we're going to discuss the types of rods, their characteristics, and what rod to use for what situation.

The rod is effectively a catapult for the bait. Since your bait needs to be cast to certain swims with perfect presentation, you need to learn what makes a rod work the way it does. If not, how are you going to know which rod suits your style of fishing? Essentially, there are three main things that manufacturers use to classify rods. They are action, test curves, and rod length. If you know what type of fish you're hoping to catch, the size of fish you're targeting and also the style of fishing you will be doing you can choose your rod accordingly.

Rod Action

The rod action refers to the degree of bending that your rod can undergo when you cast it, and the time it takes to return to its neutral position. It's the most critical aspect of your fishing rod as it determines how far and how well you'll be able to cast your bait and how much power you will have over fighting carp. Rod action mostly depends on the material the manufacturers use to create the rod and often on the weight of the bait and rig you're using. You might notice that your rod is not acting as it should when you cast it with a lighter or heavier weight attached than the one the rod action specifies it for.

Rod action is classified into several types, ranging from fast to slow, with mixed action rods such as medium-fast in between. So, let's get to the meaty part and discuss what these rods do.

Fast Action Rods

Fast action rods are also known as tip action rods. These rods are usually manufactured with experienced anglers in mind. Fast action rods have a lot less give and tend to return to their original shape much faster than other rods. These qualities give this rod some excellent casting abilities and lots of power to manoeuvre large and powerful fish: making these rods harder to control or influence.

With fast action rods, you'll see that most of the rod remains straight when you cast except the tip. The tip will bend to almost 90 degrees and help you cast to huge distances. This characteristic comes from the stiff quality of the rod that acts as an excellent catapult for your line. Most anglers use fast-action rods to reel in very large fish or fish that you might find in exceptionally weedy areas. When you pair fast action rods with heavy weights, you'll be able to cast to considerable distances.

Word to the wise — fast action rods can cause hook pulls if you don't adjust your movements according to the situation because they're very stiff and don't have a lot of give. Remember what we said about fast action rods being good for experienced anglers? This situation is what we meant!

Medium Action Rods

Medium action rods are a little slower and a little less stiff than fast action rods. Also called middle to top action rods, you'll see that these rods are comparatively easier for beginners to handle. As their name describes, the top half of the rod bends with the weight as you cast the line. Medium action rods also take a little more time to return to their original position.

Ask any angler, and they'll tell you — the most outstanding quality of the medium action rods is their versatility. Whether you want to fish for reasonable large or small carp, this rod should give you just enough control over the fish while giving enough rigidity to cast medium to light rigs. If you're just starting out or have trouble casting well, you might need to invest in a good quality medium-action rod. With its intermediate casting distance and greater bending capability, this rod allows you to fight carp at close ranges. Since this rod has a lot more give as compared to fast action rods, there's a much smaller chance of hook pulls and lost fish.

Slow Action Rods

Slow action rods bend all the way through the entire length of the rod. These rods are called slow action because they take quite a bit of time to return to their original position after you cast them. These rods tend to give the carp plenty of time before going back to neutral. They're also called through action, which refers to the way they bend through their entire lengths all the way to the rod handles.

Slow action rods are wonderful for preventing hook pulls. Since this rod bends right down to the handle, it's give prevents the hook from getting popped out of the carp's mouth as it struggles and fights. These rods are also a lot more sensitive so that you will feel each pull and push of your carp's struggle with the bending of the rod. This sensitivity and reduced rigidity of the rod comes at a cost of losing power to fight hard fighting or large fish.

Another critical aspect of slow-action rods is their casting distance. If you're dreaming of casting your line some hundred yards away with the help of slow action rods, let us tell you that's not possible. Slow action rods are only useful for casting in close quarters, so if you intend to fish close by to where you're standing, slow action rods are the ones for you. If not, you might need to invest in a stiffer rod to help you cast farther.

Test Curves

Do you ever wonder how much weight your rod can withstand before it breaks? We're going to give you the lowdown on test curves and why it's so vital that you know all about it.

Many beginner anglers return from tackle shops empty-handed and confused because they can't figure out which test curve rod to buy. Essentially, the test curve is an effective measure of how strong your fishing rod is. It is just a measure of how much weight your rod needs to bear to bend from its neutral position to a 90° angle. So, if you hold your 3 lb fishing rod horizontally and attach a 3 lb weight to it, it's going to bend to 90° in the direction of the weight.

However, measuring test curves is not an accurate science. You now know the literal definition of a test curve is the amount of weight the rod needs to bend to a right angle. However, when you approach the 90° mark, you're going to need to add more and more weight to make the rod bend, which means the rod does not uniformly bend under the weight. This situation, along with the differences in materials used in making fishing rods, causes a lot of confusion in how the test curves affect the action of the rods.

In any case, test curves are still one of the most accurate ways to measure the mode of action of some fishing rods, so anglers are sticking to it for now. Let's see what the different types of most common test curves are used for and which one might be a good choice for you.

3-lb Test Curves

These test curves usually describe rods on the stiffer side of the spectrum. They are excellent for fishing over large distances with medium to heavy rigs and will help you cast accurately even if you're aiming for a far-off spot. However, some anglers might find the 3-lb test curve a little too inadequate when they're loading the line with heavy PVA bags or spods.

If you'd like to provide some support to really heavy rigs such as those, opt for a fishing rod with a higher test curve, such as the 3.5-lb or 4-lb fishing rod. Remember that heavier test curves generally aren't much help if you want to fish nearby or around the margin. In addition, the 3.5-lb test curve might cause the fishing rod to have more hook pulls than other rods.

2-2.5-lb Test Curves

These types of test curve are ideal for fishing rods you're going to use to fish on a small lake or near the margins. You'll be able to reel in relatively heavy fish with this one without worrying about hook pulls and overgunning the fish. The general rule of thumb when comparing different test curves is trying to find out what distance you're going to cast at and how heavy your bait will be. If you're going to be casting at shorter distances, the 2.5-lb fishing rod might be a great idea for you.

However, it might not be a great idea to use a 2.5-lb fishing rod if you're using PVA bags, spods or heavy feeder rigs. Since these types of baits are quite heavy, you might have trouble casting them accurately with this type of rod.

1.5-lb Test Curve

If you're fishing in small bodies of water and aiming for smaller carp while using light baits, a 1.5-lb rod might be the right thing for the job. These agile rods allow the angler to feel every bit of the carp's struggle, which allows the angler to adjust their arm movements according to the situation to ensure they don't lose the fish. These rods are great at preventing arm fatigue as well because they're much lighter than their stiffer counterparts. You won't see many people in the UK using these rods because the most commonly used test curves are 2.5-3.5-lb. However, the only way to truly learn all about test curves is to *test them out*. There's a chance you might enjoy fishing with the more sensitive 1.5-lb rod than the 3-lb crowd favourite.

Rod Length

Rod length is typically measured from the edge of the rod handle to the tip of the rod. Companies sell rods between six to thirteen feet, so you'll have quite a range to decide from when the time comes. As a general rule of thumb, longer rods help you cast longer distances and shorter rods tend to shine at close quarters. If you're fishing at the margins or planning on surface fishing, you'll do well with a short rod. However, if you're planning on going in deep, you'll need a longer fishing rod for that.

One thing to remember is that shorter stiff rod will pack more power, so if you encounter really hard fighting fish, a short rod will help you reel it in a lot more easily than a long rod. They're also lighter, so there's less of a chance of you suffering from arm fatigue at the end of the trip.

However, longer rods are much quicker, so the angler can act rapidly when they feel the carp biting. You'll also notice that the long handle and length tend to absorb some of the shock caused by the carp's movements. Most experienced anglers will tell you that you need to decide on a rod length by considering the size of the fish you're hoping to catch, the distance you're planning to cast, and how experienced you are. Our advice to beginners would be to invest in a sturdy 10-12 feet long rod with the perfect balance between strength and casting distance.

Now that we've covered the basics of fishing rods, it's time to discuss the kind of rod you'll need to buy for some specific instances. Most fishing situations require rods with different qualities for optimal results, and this section will tell you exactly what you need to look for in each rod.

Standard Carp Rods

Standard carp rods are the rods that have specifications that can aid you in a lot of carp fishing situations. Because of that, you'll need to put a lot of thought into buying a carp rod for your everyday fishing activities.

Action

The action is a combination of the rod's stiffness and elasticity which allows the rod to return to its neutral position after being deformed. It gives a good measure of what your rod will act like in real-life situations, so be sure to purchase a good quality rod. Most good quality rods have high modulus and work well with heavier, hard-fighting carp and smaller carp in serene waters.

Usually, most experienced anglers will recommend a suitable medium-action rod to you if you're just beginning your carp fishing journey which give ample control and casting ability. As you grow more experienced and want to experiment with bigger baits and target specimen carp, you can gradually make the switch to fast action rods.

Rod Types

Length

Most standard carp rods come in 10 to 13 feet lengths. The 13 feet rods have a tendency to get stuck in overhanging branches and brambles, making it a bit of a hassle to deal with.

The 10-12 feet long rods are a much better idea for newbies and seasoned anglers. These rods give you plenty of length to play the fish or cast great distances without exhausting your arm or sacrificing the agility of your rod. The great thing about the 12 feet long carp rod is that it's the best choice for carp fishing in most lakes and reservoirs as it complements their depth and works as a great rod for casting distances on typical venues that anglers frequent. You'll also be pleased to learn that the 12 feet length of the standard carp rod works well with the landing nets that you'll be using because landing nets tend to have 6 feet long handles.

Test Curves

As we've already explained, test curves measure how much weight the carp needs to have to bend to a 90° angle. For a standard carp rod, you'd do very well with a 2.75lb rod because it's light enough with enough power to control your catch, but it also has enough range for you to cast pretty far away. However, test curves are up to the angler's discretion and can be switched up according to their preferences.

For example, if an angler wishes to fish a far off swim with heavier baits, they might need to get a rod with a heavier test curve, such as a 3.5lb carp rod. If, however, the swim is close by, it's best to stick to the 2.5lb rod because of its various advantages. We say this because heavier test curves are harder to manipulate and can be tricky for beginners to work with!

Feeder Rods

Feeder rods are used for fishing with method, cage or open-ended feeder. They're great for presenting neatly packed bait at the bottom of the water, which is where carp will spend a lot of time scavenging for food. The feeders are packed with bait such as groundbait and pellets, so it's important that the feeder rod you're using can withstand this kind of weight.

Most people use method feeders because the feeder mix sticks to the method feeder until it hits the water. Then, the groundbait mix or pellet mix starts to slowly fall away, leaving a small attractive mound of bait which presents the hookbait perfectly on top (if done correctly). This cloud of slowly-releasing bait will attract nearby carp to its immediate vicinity, after which they will feed on the mound of aromatic method feeder mix and subsequently pick up hookbait presented within. This is just a brief description of feeder fishing, which we will discuss in more detail in "Chapter 6 - Rigs".

Action

Most anglers buy feeder rods that are medium action rods because their easy bending ability provides the feeder with the casting distance it requires without compromising its accuracy with enough power to fight larger carp. If you opted for a slow action feeder rod it may too pliable to cast heavier feeder rigs. At the end of the day, it depends on your skill with the rod — if you're capable of handling stiffer rods and you want to cast far away, you should opt for fast action rods. In contrast, slow action rods might be a better idea for newbie anglers who don't have the hang of feeder fishing yet and want to fish the margins with light feeder rigs.

Length

Most of the decisions you'll make regarding what kind of feeder fishing rod you need to buy depend on the type of fishing you will be doing. Are you going to be fishing for F1s and smaller carp, or are you after large specimens? Will you be fishing close to the bank or farther out? Finding a great feeder rod won't be difficult for you if you know the answer to these questions. You'll find most feeder fishing rods in the range of 9 to 13 feet in length. Your feeder rod's length corresponds with the distance it will let you cast. Typically, 9 feet long rods will let you cast as far as 30 metres away, whereas a 12-13 feet long rod will allow you to cast your feeder to a distance of up to 80 metres! Most beginners buy shorter rods to get used to the idea of feeder rods before moving to longer models.

Test Curves

Feeder rods are unique for their use of quiver tips which are special tips that quiver or shake when the rod registers a bite on the line. This quivering quality allows the rod to have an increased sensitivity when it comes to bite detection that makes it stand out from other rods. Using these tips means you don't need to get a bite alarm to find out a carp has taken the bait but you will need to keep your eye on the quiver tip. The quiver tips come in different sizes that correspond with their level of sensitivity. This level of sensitivity is the same as the test curves in standard carp rods. The weight that can bend a quiver tip through 90° is the test curve of the feeder rod. Generally, anglers use quiver tips with lighter test curves for increased sensitivity and for catching smaller carp. The lighter the test curve of your quiver tip rod, the easier it will be to find out if a carp is interacting with your bait. For example, when you see the quiver tip tremble or quiver, you can tell a carp (or other fish) is nearby.

On the other hand, if the quiver tip bends violently, you'll know that a carp is trying to pull away with your bait. However, lighter test curves are of no use when you're using the feeder rod to catch bigger carp species or when the weather is quite windy. Since they are so sensitive to movement, the wind tends to affect quiver tips with lighter test curves quite a lot. So, if you're fishing and there's no wind, and you're targeting smaller fish, you should use quiver tips with test curves between 0.5oz and 1.5oz. On the other hand, if you're hoping to reel in some huge carp and the weather is significantly windy, you'll need to use quiver tips with test curves between 2oz to 5oz.

Float Rods

Float rods are used for suspending your bait at different depths so that it's presented as an attractive package to the nearby carp. Poles, wagglers, sticks and sliding floats are typically the floats one uses while float fishing. This type of fishing is relatively common in the UK, so we definitely need to talk about this while talking about the most common types of fishing rods.

Action

Most float rods have slow action and a lot more flexibility than other types of rods. However, you'll notice that anglers switch up the action of their float rod depending on the distance to the swim and the species they're hoping to catch. For reeling in heavy, fighting fish, a medium action rod is your best bet for versatility.

Length

Float rods are longer and thinner than other types of rods because their light quality allows for them to be held for long periods. Float rods in the UK typically start at 10 feet and go up to 13 feet. By this time, you're probably scratching your head and wondering how you can remember all this information, so count yourself lucky because this tidbit is easier to remember than most. *The longer the rod, the greater the casting distance.* Shorter rods are easier to handle, allowing you to access the landing net easily. Longer rods are better for casting your float out into the distance, so it essentially depends on what part of your swim you plan on fishing in.

Test Curves

We've learnt by now that using heavier baits means you need to use fishing rods with bulkier test curves. However, you don't need to do any such thing when it comes to float rods. If you try to fish the swim with a 3-lb test curve float rod, you're going to have some issues casting light float rigs. The rigid structure of 3-lb rods doesn't accommodate casting light rigs very will, and all your work will go to waste. In this situation, your best bet is a float rod with a test curve in the range of 1.75lb to 2.5lb. With these float rods, you're going to be able to cast closeish distance with just enough power to catch reasonably sized carp

Spod Rods

Spod rods are fishing rods you use when you want to bait your swim with spods. Spods are plastic rockets filled with baits such as micropellets, groundbait, worms, breadcrumbs or a mixture of baits resulting in an attractive combination for the carp. The spods have a nose made of buoyant material that tips the contents of the spod when it hits the water to tip all the delicious goodies that carp love. If you're worried about the accuracy of your cast, there's no need. Reels come equipped with line clips that allow the angler to cast in precisely the same place as the last time. Now, let's see what the specifications for an excellent spod rod are.

Action

Spod rods have progressive action, which essentially means that they work mainly as a tip action or fast action rod when there is a light load. However, when you increase the load, the rod evenly distributes the weight, thus balancing the weight between the rod's tip, middle, and butt.

Length

Most spod rods are sold within the range of 12 to 13 feet length. These lengths are ideal for baiting distant spots in your swim with large amounts of bait without exhausting your arm with a stick or catapult. Most beginners opt for 12 feet rods because they provide a good balance between excellent casting ability and easy manoeuvring. If you're one of those anglers who love baiting far off areas of the lake that you're fishing in, you'll love using spod rods because a 12-13 feet spod rod will effectively bait a spot that's far from you.

Test Curves

Test curves make a lot of difference when we talk about heavier baits such as spods or spombs. Since these plastic rockets are loaded with bait, you're going to need a spod rod with a strong test curve to back them up. Most anglers usually use spod rods with a test curve of 3.5lb to withstand the weight of the spods. However, when you want to cast your bait to a distance of 90 metres or more, you're going to need a spod rod with a greater test curve, such as 4.5lb or 5lb.

So, now that we've concluded the section on carp fishing rods, we hope you've learnt enough from it to choose a suitable rod for your carp fishing adventures. Another very critical aspect of carp fishing is choosing the right reel. Half your work is done for you if you choose the right reel after selecting the right rod. But don't worry, we're also going to help you polish your carp fishing techniques later in the book, in addition to discussing the various essential aspects of carp fishing tackle!

Components Of A Carp Fishing Reel

A good carp fishing reel is critical to your success as an angler, and the first step to mastering the science behind these reels and choosing a suitable one for yourself is to learn all about the inner workings of the carp fishing reels. This exercise includes learning about gear ratios, ball bearings, line capacities, reel sizes, and handles, among other things. In this section, we will be discussing the various components of fishing reels.

Line Capacity

Line capacity is the easiest of the lot to remember. As its name indicates, the line capacity of a carp fishing reel measures the length of line that you can wrap around the spool of the reel. Most standard carp fishing reels hold up to 200 metres of line, while big pit reels hold a lot more line than that. Reels with huge line capacities are typically called big pit reels. Anglers use big pit reels to catch those huge specimen carp because the abundance of line allows you to work on your catch without worrying about how much your reel is oscillating or if you're going to run out. The bigger spools on the big pit reels also help decrease friction when you're casting the line and creating a better line lay.

On the other hand, beginners tend to use free spool reels when fishing once in a while because this type of reel strips itself of the line so you can set your rod in an alarm and not have to worry about the carp stripping your rod into the water before you get to it. You can halt the stripping if you detect a bite by turning the handle of the free spool reel. Free spool reels weigh a lot less than big pit reels. That means if you're going to be spodding all day, you might want to pick up a free spool reel to prevent fatiguing your arm.

Bearings

This part of fishing reels is relatively easy to explain. Bearings decrease friction and increase the smoothness of the movement associated with reeling in your catches. There are several types of ball bearings that you may find in your reels, such as corrosion-resistant bearings, roller bearings or ball bearings. Bearings prevent your reel from suffering wear and tear while you reel in your catches. It also decreases the struggle associated with reeling in when friction or trapped particles cause your reel to have a rough feel. However, bearings don't just make your life easier when you're reeling in your catch. It's also a tremendous help when you're casting the line, which means you owe much of your precise casting to the presence of bearings in your fishing reels.

Gear Ratio

The gear ratio, also called the cranking power, is a measure of how much line is reeled in with every 360° turn of the spool. When you see a manufacturer advertising the gear ratio of a particular reel as 5.2:1, it means that the spool rotates 5.2 times for every single complete turn of the reel handle. These days, most gear ratios range between 5.2:1 to 7.0:1, with most anglers opting for the reels with the gear ratios of 5.2:1 and 6.2:1. The gear ratio is essentially a measure of the speed with which your reel retrieves the line. That is why most experienced anglers opt for high-speed models such as the 7.0:1 because they know it's easier to work with a high-speed model than with one in which you have to crank the reel to get a fast retrieve manually. Reels such as the ones you use for spod rods will need you to do a lot of reeling in very fast, so it's best to choose a reel with a high gear ratio for your spod reel.

Reel Size

Like all things, reels come in a variety of sizes, and what kind of fish you're going to be catching on it will have a lot of bearing on what type of reel size you ought to be buying. You'll see some reels advertised as sizes that are in the thousands, such as 6000, 7000 and 12000, whereas other reels are described as having sizes 060, 070, 080. However, there's no need to panic because the two size styles are easy enough to figure out. A size 020 usually means a size 2000, while a size 035 means a size 3500 fishing reel. Most anglers use reel sizes in the range of 5000 to 8000 when fishing for carp. These sizes hold a fair lot of line and tend to be quite powerful for reeling in strong, struggling carp.

Handles

Handles are another essential part of fishing reels. Most companies offer reels in single or double styles. You'll notice that single handles turn better and provide smooth movements when you're reeling in a big carp, while double handles are a lot easy to turn because of the distribution of the effort on both sides. Handles may be made from wood, plastic or metal and may have different feels depending on what manufacturer you're buying from. This part of reel shopping is entirely up to the angler's discretion and doesn't involve much science behind it.

Line Clips

Line clips are a critical part of carp fishing reels, especially when you're fishing a prebaited swim, using feeders or baiting a spot with spods or spombs. Line clips allow the angler to clip the line at the length at which they wish to cast the line. It delivers great accuracy while casting because the angler can cast the line at precisely the spot they previously prebaited or the spot where they've been sending spods for the past hour. It's also helpful for holding your line when you're moving your equipment from one spot to another, but it mostly shines in situations when you need your casting distance to be precise.

Carp Fishing Lines

This section deals with another all-important aspect of carp fishing: choosing which fishing line to use. Before, anglers only had a monofilament line to catch carp with; now, there's a more extensive variety. This variety also means that anglers need to do their research before opting for one type of fishing line to use on their angling adventures.

Line Strength

The line strength of a carp is a measure of how much weight it can bear without breaking. It is measured in lb, and manufacturers also call it the breaking strength of the line. The rule of thumb when choosing between line strengths is that the higher the line strength, the heavier the carp that you'll be able to catch with it. You'll see that fishing lines actually advertise line strengths as low as 1lb, but those are for really small silver fish that the line will easily be able to reel in without breaking. For carp, you need to look in the range of 10lb to around 30lb. This range is usually sufficient to catch most carp. In addition, you'll need fishing lines with large line strengths when you're fishing in weedy water or where there's a high chance of the line getting snagged on something.

Types Of Fishing Lines

There are three main types of fishing lines that carp anglers usually choose between. These are monofilament, fluorocarbon and braided. They all have their strengths and their weaknesses, which is why we'll do an overview of what situation each type of fishing line is used for.

Monofilament

Monofilament, also called mono, is one of the most common fishing lines. Manufacturers mostly make monofilament lines from nylon, but they can be made from other materials as well. It has a lot of elasticity so that it can give your carp a lot of room for fighting. In addition, its small diameter also ensures that it holds knots quite well. It's also usually strong enough for most carp species, so if you're looking for a simple line to use for some basic carp fishing, monofilament is an excellent choice. It also floats quite well, so mono is an ideal choice for surface fishing. However, since it floats well, it's not good for bottom fishing because it doesn't sink all that well. If you are fishing heavy rigs this won't be an issue anyway. This line does have some memory, which means it may develop some irritating curves or kinks if it sits in the spool for a long time.

Fluorocarbon

Fluorocarbon is similar to monofilament in terms of diameter, but it's made from a material that is practically invisible underwater. If you're fishing in very clear waters or the carp species you're hoping to catch is easily spooked, fluorocarbon is a great choice. It also has a very smooth texture which allows it to be extremely abrasion-resistant as the silky texture allows it to slide over snags and weeds without getting stuck. You'll get very precise casting with fluorocarbon lines because it only stretches under high pressure, allowing you to get mono's elasticity but with greater precision. If you let it go slack, you'll learn that it easily sinks to the bottom, making it an ideal choice for presenting bait at the bottom or float rigs where you want the bait and line to sink. However, make sure that you clean your fluorocarbon line from time to time because it can accumulate dirt on its surface, making it lose the invisibility factor of fluorocarbon lines. While it is essentially a perfect line, its only downside is that some knots don't stay on as tightly on fluorocarbon lines as they do on monofilament ones.

Braided

A braided line is created by meshing together several separate strands. This process gives braided lines superior strength while maintaining the thin diameter that anglers love in mono and fluorocarbon lines. It's also quite resistant to abrasion like fluorocarbon. In addition, it has virtually no memory, which means you won't have to straighten out any annoying kinks when fishing with a braided line. This type of fishing line also doesn't stretch a lot, which means that you'll need to switch up the test curve of your rod if you want more give in your setup. It's excellent for bite detection and casting accurately because of its rigid makeup. This line can also withstand greater weights while having almost the same diameter as before, which is an excellent point for braided lines. You'll learn that braided lines are a perfect option for fishing in waters where there's a lot of vegetation and low visibility.

The equipment that you attach to the end of your fishing line is called end tackle. It includes a variety of things in it, from feeders and hooks to floats and weights and much more. You need to keep in mind six main types of end tackle, which we will now discuss.

Hooks

Hooks are a small but critical part of your fishing rig. You need to make sure that the hook you attach to your line is suitable for the situation and the fish you're hoping to catch. We need to discuss several types of fishing hooks, but before that, let's briefly overview the essential parts of a hook's anatomy.

The point of the hook is the sharp end that pierces into the carp's mouth. There's a spike projecting from the point that goes backwards, which is called the barb. It prevents the hook from disengaging from the carp's mouth when it struggles. The bend of the hook is the part that curves downward. The section of the hook that connects the point to the bend is called the throat of the hook. The eye is the part of the hook that serves as the point of attachment between the fishing line and the hook that you're attaching to. The section that connects the eye to the bend is called the shank. The degree of space or distance between the throat and the shank is called the gape of the hook. If you have all these definitions down, let's progress to the different types of fishing hooks that you'll encounter.

Long Shank

Long shank hooks are typically long and thin, which makes them ideal for fishing near the bottom. We all know carp are bottom-feeders, which is why these hooks are pretty useful to catch some hungry carp. However, its long length can sometimes cause the bait to be pushed to the opposite end of the point. You can overcome this problem by using a piece of tubing to make it stay in place. However, this hook is not used a lot by carp anglers these days.

Curved Shank

If you see some common hooks up close, you'll see that they all have straight shanks. This type of shank is popular for the curved quality of its shank. This characteristic makes it much harder for the struggling carp to disengage the hook from its mouth. While curved shank hooks were previously used for fly fishing, carp anglers have also started using them in recent years.

Wide Gape

As their name indicates, wide gape hooks typically have a large space between the throat and the shank. This space makes it difficult for the fish to eject the hook from its mouth when it struggles. This type of hook works very well in the bottom as well as surface fishing. If you want a hook that's suitable for nearly all fishing situations, you should opt for a wide gape hook.

Stiff Rigger

Instead of an in-turned eye, stiff rigger hooks have an out-turned eye. Since they're great to use with chod rigs, many people also call them chod hooks now. Back in the day, monofilament and fluorocarbon lines wouldn't perform very well when tied to a hook with an in-turned eye, which gave birth to the idea of the stiff rigger. This type of hook is very popular among anglers these days for how well it works with more rigid lines such as those of the fluorocarbon variety.

Weights

Weights, or leads, as most anglers call them, are a type of end tackle that you attach to your rig to make sure that the rig sinks to the bottom and holds itself in place. Weight also allow the hook to sink firmly into the carp's mouths the carp tries to run with your bait and weight on your rig. Most anglers use weights in the range of 1-3oz for carp fishing, with lighter weights in calmer weather and casting close and heavier weights in windier weather and for casting far. While there are several subtypes of weights, there are two main types that you need to understand.

In-Line Weights

As their name describes, the line weaves directly through this type of weight. You'll see that the weight has a hole running through its centre, which allows the line to pass through it. It's ideal for presenting bait at different depths and can help you cast accurately over a distance greater than 70 meters. Feeder, flat pear, tournament, and gripper leads are typically available as in-line weights.

Swivel Weights

As their weight indicates, swivel weights have a swivel that helps them attach to the fishing line. Your mainline does not pass through the weight in this type of lead as it did in the in-line weights. Gripper, pear, flat pear, and marker leads are some types of swivel weights.

Feeders

Feeders are small plastic capsules that anglers pack bait on or in. These baits can be groundbait mixes, pellets or other kinds of aromatic baits which attract the carp to the hookbait hidden within the mix. Feeder fishing is a major branch of carp fishing because of the accuracy with which you can bait your swim and the great presentation that your bait has at the bottom of the water. Since carp are bottom-feeders, anglers love to reel them in with the help of these little plastic capsules of bait. They usually use four major feeders while fishing for carp: method feeders, open-ended feeders, cage feeders, and maggot feeders.

Method Feeder

This type of feeder is easily the most commonly used feeder among anglers. All you need to do is use the mould given with the feeder to pack your bait mix on it uniformly with the hookbait hidden in between. Once the perfectly mixed bait is compact onto your feeder, you fish your swim with it. The method feeder always falls bottom-first onto the floor of the lake, and its flat bottom makes sure that the bait on top starts to disperse, so that nearby hungry carp come in from the surrounding areas to feed and find your hookbait presented in the mound of free offerings.

End Tackle

Maggot Feeder

Maggots are traditional favourites among UK anglers because you always have a chance to attract some carp and other fish with this tasty bait. A maggot feeder is basically a small metal or plastic container with holes punched into it that allows you to transport a lot of maggots to your swim in one go. These maggots wriggle out of the holes in the feeder, thereby attracting nearby carp to them.

Open-Ended Feeder

As its name indicates, the open-ended feeder is a small cylinder that's open from both sides. Anglers usually pack it with groundbait and use it in situations where you want your bait to be released slowly.

Cage Feeder

The cage feeder is a metal can made out of mesh, making it look like a cage. Anglers use it for fishing shallow swims because the meshwork allows the bait to be released rapidly. This speed enables anglers to fish much faster than they would with other feeder types.

Floats

A float is a type of end tackle that anglers use for float fishing. It allows anglers to suspend their bait at a certain depth in the water. Floats are used when anglers are targeting carp that one usually finds in intermediate water depths. There are three different types of floats that carp anglers use in their fishing adventures. They are waggler, stick, and controller floats.

Waggler

Waggler floats are the ones that you attach to the end of the line. They are pretty sensitive and excellent for float fishing in calm water commercial venues of the UK. Wagglers come in two different types — straight and bodied. This float type is relatively cheap and one of the most commonly used in carp fishing.

Controller

Controller floats are excellent for bite detection and controlling how far out you cast your line. Since they are weighted, you'll be able to cast them much further than other floats. They have a swivel at the top, and they also serve as a visual indication of when you have a bite like other floats.

Stick

Stick floats are held in place with the help of three different silicone or rubber attachments at the top, centre, and bottom of the float. Since most UK anglers opt for serene lakes, fisheries, and reservoirs, you won't see a lot of stick floats while fishing here because these floats are traditionally used for fast-flowing waters such as rivers.

Tubing

Tubing is an essential part of your carp fishing rig. It's typically a long hollow tube made out of PVC or tungsten that you slip on before attaching your lead and hook link. Hook links can get tangled up with the mainline at times which creates quite a mess. To avoid that, anglers use hollow tubing, which is not prone to tangling. It's also a vital part of a safe carp fishing rig because there's a chance of the carp getting hurt if it comes in contact with the line without tubing, resulting in lost scales or more serious injuries. Manufacturers usually sell tubing in a variety of colours that easily blend into the underwater surroundings.

Swivels

Swivels are typically used as a connection between the mainline and the hook link. These swivels have rotating rings at each end with a joint in between, ensuring that the line doesn't break or twist too much when you're trying to reel in a catch or playing the carp. There are three main types of swivels that anglers use for carp fishing: ball bearing swivels, barrel swivels, and crane swivels.

Ball Bearing Swivel

This swivel type is typically the most expensive one because it works well under a variety of conditions. The ball bearing swivel rotates freely because the ball bearing's presence ensures no friction in the arrangement. You'll be able to work very big fish and heavy loads with this kind of swivel.

Barrel Swivel

The barrel swivel is the cheapest of the lot and is the one many anglers use in their rigs. However, it can't rotate freely if you hook a big catch or there's a heavy load attached to it.

Crane Swivel

The crane swivel provides an intermediate degree of rotation between the barrel and the ball bearing swivels. It works better under heavy loads as compared to the barrel swivel but doesn't rotate as freely as the ball bearing swivel.

Rubber Beads

Rubber beads are an essential part of most carp fishing rigs as they protect the knot from damage and also make sure that the lead does not interact with the mainline. Most carp anglers use rubber beads in chod and helicopter rigs. These soft beads fit snugly over silicone tubing and work as great shock absorbers in various setups.

Float Stops

Float stops are small beads made out of rubber that stop your float from sliding down the mainline all the way to the end of the line. This rubber stopper ensures that you can present your float at a depth of your choice, with the float sliding away on the line.

Safety Weight Clips

Safety weight clips are a part of terminal tackle that serve purposes for both the fish and the angler. The weights hang from these weight clips, ensuring that things don't go sideways if the line gets snagged in vegetation. When the lead gets tangled in something, it exerts some pressure on the weight clip. The pressure makes the weight clip release the weight, allowing the angler to continue on as if nothing happened. In addition, it's also helpful in case you suffer a breakage in the mainline. Breakages happen when the line is under too much tension, so everyone needs to use safety weight clips because they ensure that the carp don't get stuck dragging a weight if your weight gets caught and the line snaps.

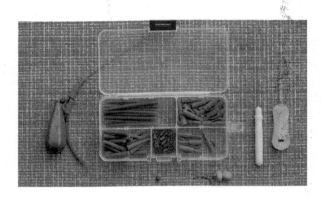

Carp fishing requires its own specialised set of tools that you need to ensure that your carp fishing rig is in its best possible shape. You've probably seen most of these tools before on your fishing trips, which is why this section will be relatively easy to digest!

Bait Needle

Bait needle is an incredibly useful tool when it comes to putting baits on hair rigs. While many anglers are opting for pre-tied rigs, some anglers tie their own rigs. You'll need a bait needle to pierce your bait and attach it to the hair in the rig. There are many different types of bait needles such as standard, close lip, splicing and braid needles.

Bait Drill

A bait drill is a simple tool that allows you to drill out baits to fix on hair rigs. It looks like a small drill bit and helps you clear a hole in your bait when you start rotating it inside the bait.

Pellet Bander

A pellet bander will be your best friend when you wish to hook a pellet that is not predrilled onto a hair rig. This handy tool helps you attach your pellet to the band by a simple method that allows you to save time and avoid the struggle of having the pellet slip from your hands again and again as you try to band it. All you need to do is insert the pellet into the pellet bander and close it. Your pellet will be banded when it emerges out!

Bait Bands

Bait bands are basically small bands made out of rubber that help you attach hard baits like pellets to your hook. You just slide the band connected to the hook onto the pellet with your hand or your pellet bander, and you're all set to fish with a hard bait!

Boilie Spikes

Boilie spikes are little needle-like pieces of plastic that have spikes on them. They help to secure the boilie to the hook. All you need to do is insert a baiting needle clean through your soft boilie so that it comes out of the other side and then take it out. In its place, insert the boilie spike so that it fits snugly inside the boilie. Trim off the extra edge that emerges from the other side, and you're good to go!

Rig Puller

Rig puller, also called the knot puller, is a tool anglers use to secure their knots and make sure they are as tight as possible. You just insert one end of the line in the hook on the rig puller and pull it as hard as you can while holding the other end of the line in your other hand.

Loop Tier

A loop tier is a very useful tool that helps you tie loops with exactly the same diameter as before. It's great for making sure your lengths are accurate but also because it offers a more convenient way to tie a sturdy loop that doesn't involve fiddling with the line with your hands.

Watercraft

Watercraft

A lot of anglers will tell you that carp fishing is a hit-and-miss hobby. Some days, you get plenty of carp on the bank, whereas you struggle to catch even a single carp on other days. However, that's not the case. You've just located a good spot on the lake in good conditions on the days when you get a lot of catches.

But how can you make sure that you get a good spot every time you head out for a spot of fishing? The art of spotting an excellent fishing spot in your swim is called watercraft. It is a combination of spotting visual signs, learning a venue, knowing how weather conditions affect the carp, how to spot carp patrol routes and the role of bottom composition in carp behaviour.

Watercraft also includes decoding different carp behaviours to understand when the perfect time to fish them is. These behaviours include carp jumping, rolling and patrolling. This section will talk about all the basics of watercraft — spotting signs of carp, features, and understanding the weather and water quality.

The first aspect of watercraft is spotting where the carp are feeding or are present. You need to keep your eye out for these visible features because nine times out of ten, baiting the part of the swim that has these characteristics will help you reel in some nice carp. Contrary to what some people may tell you, watercraft is not a natural instinct. Instead, it is honed by years of practice and learning what works. The following characteristics will give you all the information you'll need about watercraft.

Bubbles

Carp release bubbles of gas from their gills when they sort through the silt to differentiate between edible and inedible items. Carp also release bubbles of air from their swim bladders when they ascend in the water. Most experienced anglers say bubbles produced by large carp species are usually large but short-lived, whereas small carp species such as crucian carp produce tiny foam-like bubbles when they scavenge for food.

An excellent way to know whether the carp are feeding in an area of the swim is to check if there are any noticeable bubbles around that place. Most anglers like to stay prepared and keep a baited rod nearby in case they see any bubbles rising to the surface, which will indicate the presence of some hungry carp in the vicinity.

Carp Jumping

Another great way to determine what part of the swim is a good feeding ground for the carp is to check if there are any carp breaching the water surface at any point. If you see the carp jumping out of the water, it usually means that they are feeding in the silt below and need to clear their gills by hitting the water with some force. Areas where the carp do that are excellent places to cast.

However, if you see the carp making some rolling motions on the surface, it doesn't indicate that there are any carp feeding in that area. This movement usually tells us that the carp are migrating elsewhere.

Mud Clouds And Floating Debris

Another tell-tale sign of carp feeding at the bottom is the presence of mud clouds or floating debris such as pulled up weeds or other aquatic vegetation. When the bottom of the lake is silty, you'll see the water getting cloudy when the carp feed at the bottom. This phenomenon is usually referred to as mud clouds. On the other hand, when the bottom is weedy, the carp will probably pull up some of the vegetation when it scavenges for food. This vegetation will float to the top, giving you a good idea of where the carp are. The presence of aquatic vegetation is usually a great help because moving reeds and vibrating stems also alert the angler to the presence of carp nearby.

Bird Life

If you see some startled birds, there's a good chance that there are carp nearby. For example, if you see birds such as seagulls diving towards the water to steal some floating bait or munch on some hatching insects, but they suddenly get spooked, there's a chance that they spotted some carp in the water. You'll notice them getting spooked if they rapidly change direction or hit the water in an awkward manner and immediately take off again. If you see birds munching on some insects out on the water, it means there could be quite a few carp present as well because carp love to feed on hatching insects.

Geese and swan don't have very dramatic reactions to carp the way other birds do, but they do change direction and carefully go around the carp while keeping their eyes on it when they spot one. You should pay attention to the reaction of these birds when they're moving past a weedy area or a feature such as overhanging trees. Their startled reaction will alert you to the presence of carp in the vicinity.

Patrol Routes

Carp use patrol routes to go from one natural feeding ground to another. While many anglers consider figuring out patrol routes to be a very important part of watercraft, others consider it a plus point but nothing more. There are a few ways in which you can figure out carp patrol routes. One of them goes thus: You get yourself a pair of polarised sunglasses, lather yourself in sunblock and climb up a tree overlooking the swim you will be fishing in. It will probably take you all day, but you'll probably see some repetitive movements in the water. These movements will give you a fair idea of the parts of the swim that the carp pass by when going between feeding grounds. In clear water, you'll see a lone carp or a school of carp going along a route which you should keep in mind for future reference. A bit extreme yes, but if you're serious about catching fish this can be extremely useful.

Another way to figure out carp patrol routes is to sit and wait by the margins. Since you'll be closer to the water, you'll be better able to see movement in the water. You should also strain your eyes and ears for signs of bubbles or the rustling of vegetation, which might help you know that a carp is passing by. These movements are especially frequent at dusk and dawn because of the changing quality of the light. You'll be able to figure out carp patrol routes by watching the water for a few days and noting down the places that see a lot of carp traffic. Carp are creatures of habit, so there's a high chance that they're frequenting this route to reach a food spot. When you cast the line along these routes, you'll have a much higher chance of getting a bite than when you cast blindly.

However, if you're only fishing a swim for a day or two, there isn't much chance of you figuring out the patrol routes. Another thing to remember is that it's almost impossible to figure out patrol routes in murky water because of the low visibility.

Bottom Composition

As the name indicates, the bottom composition consists of the material that the bottom of the swim is made of. Experienced anglers and beginners often overlook this aspect of watercraft because they don't think the bottom composition has a lot of bearing on how many catches you get at a particular location. However, we often tell newbies that a surefire way to have a disappointing fishing trip is not to pay attention to a particular swim's characteristics. The reason behind this is that you need to adopt different types of strategies to fish different types of bottoms. For example — you need to make sure that you fish weedy bottoms with chod rigs, whereas you can present your bait any other way on hard bottoms. Most often, anglers divide bottom compositions into two types — hard bottoms and soft bottoms.

Hard Bottom

Sand, clay and gravel are typically the components of a hard bottom lake. It's comparatively easier to fish in these lakes because the bait presents nicely against the hard, flat surface. It also contains some nooks and crannies that allow carp to hide or scavenge for food in, because hard bottoms usually harbour a greater variety of natural food sources as compared to soft bottoms. The carp also love to scavenge for food in the compact sand, which is another plus point and a major reason anglers love fishing in hard bottom lakes.

Soft Bottom

Soft bottom lakes usually consist of silt which causes the bait to sink into its depth, making it unattractive to the carp. Not only does the silt ruin the bait's presentation, but it also contains debris that makes it an unlikely place for carp to feed in. An excellent place for carp to hide in is a transitional area, which is the spot where the soft bottom changes into the hard bottom or vice versa. These places usually contain a lot of food sources, which is why you might find a lot of carp there. You can use marker floats, underwater cameras or feel the lead down to get a better idea of what the bottom composition of a particular swim is like. However, marker floats and the like tend to spook the fish, so it's better to do this during the close season or on days when you aren't going to be actually fishing there.

Features

Casting your line in a swim you've been to a hundred times before is great because you know every nook and cranny there is to know in that place. However, it's even more fun to fish in a swim that you've never been to before because it allows you to really flex your watercraft muscles and figure out what part of the lake holds the greatest number of hungry carp. Features are the parts of the lake that usually hold natural food sources for carp to fish in. They're also great places for carp to hide in because they have shadowy corners or dark nooks that the carp feel safe in. Whenever you're visiting a new lake, keep an eye out for the following features because you'll get a lot of great catches when you cast your line there.

Overhanging Trees

The great thing about this feature is that you don't need to expend a lot of energy looking for them because you'll encounter them presence at nearly every lake or venue you visit. The shade cast by the overhanging trees on the lake tricks the carp into thinking that they are safe from all sorts of disturbances. In addition, you'll see fewer people ducking under low-hanging branches to cast thier line which is why the carp imagine that they are safe there. Another reason for the higher carp population under these trees is that any fruit or vegetation that falls from these trees serves as food for the carp. These reasons are why you'll see that casting your line in the water below the overhanging branches will get you a comparatively larger number of bites.

Gravel Bars

Fishing gravel bars is an excellent way to potentially increase your catch rates because a gravel bar in open water is an ideal carp patrol route. When you feel the tell-tale tap-tap-tap on your marker rod, you know you've found a gravel bar. The carp love gravel bars because they're an excellent source of natural food and are a good spot for scratching themselves after an entire winter spent covered in leeches or other such irritants. If you fish along the borders of the bar, you're almost guaranteed to get quite a few great catches if there is carp in the area.

Margins

The most straightforward feature that you need to fish in is the margins of the lake. If you've found a spot where there aren't too many anglers around, the margin might be an ideal location to fish because the carp find enough food there to consider it a part of their patrol route but haven't seen enough rigs to be spooked. These spots are also great for anglers who struggle with long-distance casting. Just make sure to wear clothes that blend into the scenery and do not make any sudden movements or loud noises because it might spook the nearby carp.

Weeds

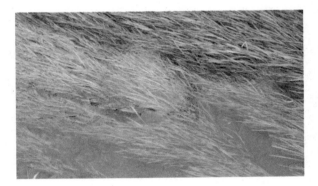

While it is rather difficult to fish in a weedy area, it's definitely worth a try. Why is that? Well, the carp love any area that's shadowy, warm, and full of vegetation and weedy areas definitely fit the bill very well! In addition, weeds and vegetation also release some oxygen that the carp love being around. Another reason why weeds are a good feature to look out for is that most newbie anglers don't cast in weeds which ensures that the carp in that area aren't spooked by rigged baits. However, it is a little tricky to fish in weedy areas, so make sure that you use a chod rig or any other setup that you think won't easily tangle in the vegetation.

Open Water

Most anglers think that 'features' refer to some obviously identifiable elements present on the lake. Instead, features are any place where you might have a better chance of catching some carp. To that end, open water is a feature we surely can't ignore because, in a place where most anglers are casting 120 yards on large venues, you casting 150 yards into the open water can work. Doing so will allow you to cast in a spot that isn't baited regularly, meaning the carp won't be as wary in that area. In addition, a far-out spot in the water is an ideal spot for carp to swim out to when they wish to escape the rigged baits present in the margins,

Islands

Islands are easily recognisable features that are an old favourite among the carp. Whether it is patrolling along its borders or scavenging for food in its sides, there's a very high chance of carp hanging around the islands present in your lake. However, since islands are quite a popular casting spot among anglers too, there's a chance that you might have tough competition when it comes to hooking into the biggest carp.

Snags

Snags can be some aquatic vegetation or fallen trees that carp usually hide around to get away from the noise and baited rigs of the margins. It's a little tricky to fish within snags, but it's well worth the effort because anglers usually find quite a few carp within the snags. However, make sure that you cast *near* the snag and not directly in it because the latter might cause you to lose the fish and the bait into the snags.

Weather

Weather is another all-important aspect of watercraft that some anglers typically forget to talk about because they get too caught up in talking about patrol routes and features. However, it plays a critical role in deciding how the fish act on a particular day and where they will head to, so it's very important for an angler to know all about it. The weather includes different things such as the temperature, the direction of the wind, the air pressure and the presence or absence of the rain. Some vigilant anglers even take the moon phases into account when planning their fishing trips!

Temperature

This one is the most obvious indicator of carp movement. When the temperatures drop, you'll have trouble finding carp by the margins because the margins are shallow, and they cool down much faster than the deeper parts of the lake. In such scenarios, you'll have better luck if you cast farther out into the lake in the open water. However, suppose you have a warm day followed by a cold night — you'll be able to find the carp by the margins just the same because water cools down much slower than air, and the carp will probably be feeding instead of snoozing because of the cold.

Winds

We often talk about angling being a multifaceted sport. One sees that demonstrated in times like these when we talk about all the things you need to know before setting out on your fishing trip. One such thing is the wind quality. It doesn't matter how fast the wind is blowing because all we need to know for our fishing trip is the *direction* it is blowing in and the temperature the direction causes it to have. Generally speaking, the wind direction is important because it affects the movement of the carp. If the wind is warm in cold weather, the carp tend to follow it. If the wind is cold in cold weather, the carp will likely go in the opposite direction to escape the chill.

Southwest winds are typically quite warm, which makes the carp swim in their direction. On the other hand, northeast winds are generally cold, which is why the carp swim opposite to its direction. Before baiting your swim, use a compass to figure out where the north of the lake bed is because it'll help you figure out the rest of the directions. Wind directions make it easier for anglers to find carp in a specific place because they usually gather in a single place to either escape the cold wind or bask in the warm one.

Air Pressure

Air pressure is another critical aspect of the weather. Generally speaking, wet, cloudy days have low pressure, whereas clear, sunny days indicate high air pressure. While you will have better visibility on high-pressure days, there won't be a lot of action in the water on those days because the oxygen concentration in the water will be low, causing the carp to get lethargic. When the sky is cloudy and wet, the pressure will be quite low, which will cause the carp to delve quite deep into the water. This will allow you to use heavier baits and have a lot of fun with playing the fish at the bottom because cloudy days see quite an increase in carp activity due to the high oxygen concentration. On days with clear skies, you should switch to lighter baits such as PVA bags and make use of floater tackle because the low pressure will cause the fish to swim close the surface. You can either look up the air pressure on the internet, make a guess by looking at the cloud cover, or even buy a barometer to keep track of the air pressure accurately.

Rain

Beginners will probably think that they won't get a lot of catches when it's raining and will sit it out. However, you should know that if you don't have a problem with a spot of rain, you'll have a great time out on the water when it's pouring because of several reasons. When it rains for a long time, you'll see a lot of silt from nearby places run into the lake. This will cause the lake to become muddy, lowering visibility by a considerable degree. While other fish species will get spooked by this development, the carp won't. In fact, they enjoy foraging in the murky water and will readily take the bait while it's raining. Another plus point that feeds their frenzy is that when it's raining, there's a lot of runoff consisting of organic matter that the carp love to munch on.

On the other hand, if you're a beginner, you'll have a lot of fun out on the water when it's raining because a lot of people don't like getting splattered with mud and rain and will probably sit it out. This situation will allow you to freely try techniques you were too scared to try in public up until now. You already know that cloud covers ensure that the air pressure will be low, causing the carp activity to be quite high.

Baits

Baits

The massive number of baits available on today's market can make choosing the best bait for carp a little confusing for all you beginner anglers. Let's be honest here, all the baits that tackle shops stock will catch carp if your fishing is correct, but there are clear winners in the bunch. Choosing the best bait for carp seems an easy task in theory, but it depends on many factors. For example, what venue you are fishing, what fishing style you opt for, the time of year, weather, and water clarity all play a significant role in which baits will work best on the day.

I know, confusing right? Not to worry, read on to find out the baits that dominate the market and are the go-to for many of us carp anglers. In this chapter, we will be talking you through all the baits you'll need, what situations they are usually fished in, and some pointers and tips when using them.

The hook baits we'll be talking you through are;

- Sweetcorn
- Boilies
- Pellets
- Pop-Ups
- Bread
- Maggots

It is without a doubt that sweet corn has its place in the top few carp fishing baits. It is highly versatile and can be used in every carp fishing session no matter what method you are fishing at every venue. Carp and plenty of other coarse fish struggle to turn away from the bright colour and sweet taste, so why would you not want to use it as bait?

Why is Sweetcorn so Good?

It seems logical to begin with why sweet corn is one of the top baits for carp fishing to get us started. One of the main reasons that sweetcorn is so good is to do with its colour. The bright yellow colour allows it to stand out exceptionally clearly in even the murkiest of waters, bringing the fish in from areas around.

Sweetcorn is top class at visually attracting hungry carp, but the salt and sugar added to tinned varieties are both excellent at attracting carp. As the salt and sugar dissolve into the water, the carp use their highly developed "olfactory" system to follow the dissolved sugar and salt and swim towards the bait. Remember, we covered this in the early sections of this book. Sweetcorn is also naturally full of amino acids proven through various studies to stimulate carp feeding. What more can you want?

Benefits of using Sweetcorn

Many benefits make sweet corn a superior bait for catching carp. Take a read at them below;

- **Easily accessible** – can be bought at nearly any store.
- **Visually attracts carp** – bright yellow colour brings carp in from the area
- **High sugar and salt content** – Carp can't resist it. Make sure to buy the tins with added sugar and salt, as some will have these additives removed.
- **Cheap** – compared to other carp baits like boilies and pellets.
- **Naturally full of amino acids** – proven to encourage carp to feed
- **Versatile** – Can be used with many carp fishing techniques

Carp Fishing Techniques with Sweetcorn

As I've said before, sweet corn is highly versatile and be used in many carp fishing situations. These include;

- Hair Rigged for any rig
- Used in method feeder mix
- Thrown into spods for baiting swims

Hair Rigged Corn

Hair rigs are commonplace in carp anglers' tackle boxes today after two well-known carp fishermen' invention in the 1980s. Hair rigs allow bait to be attached to a rig without sitting directly on the hook. This provides multiple benefits that include a natural presentation and higher chance of hooking into a fish as it explores your bait.

Sweetcorn

Hair rigs can be used with many rigs and are often the go-to for carp anglers for good presentation. These hair rigs paired with a few pieces of corn are excellent at catching carp. Sweetcorn can be attached to a hair rig quickly and easily using a bait needle and a quick stop hair rig. To do so you'll need to push the plastic stopped over the end of your bait needle and then push the stopper and needle through the sweetcorn like the picture below.

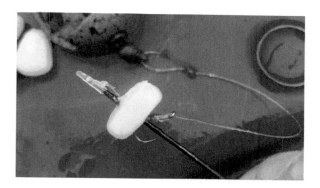

By then pulling off the stopped and pulling the bait needle back out through the sweetcorn it will be fixed on the hair rig. I would advise putting on a few pieces at a time to deter some tiny nuisance fish interested in eating the corn. These steps stand for not only sweetcorn. Any drilled pellet or boilie can be attached to a rig with the same process. Keep this in mind.

Sweetcorn in Method Feeder Mix

Another great way to use sweetcorn as bait for carp is to pour some into your feeder mix for added attraction. This can be an extremely cheap way to bait up a swim without adding too many expensive boilies, pellets and other more expensive baits than corn. Also, by adding in the liquid from the tin of corn you can add some extra salt and sugar to your mix, which will help to bring in the carp from the surrounding areas.

If you are going to be using large quantities of corn to bait up an area, you could consider buying feed corn in larger quantities. This works out as a far cheaper alternative, provides larger corn and makes baiting up large areas easier than consistently opening small cans.

Sweetcorn

Used for Spod Mix

Sweetcorn also goes excellent in spod mixes. When baiting up areas far away, you will struggle to throw or catapult sweetcorn far distances as it is relatively light. It can easily be packed into a spod with other baits such as boillies, pellets, hemp and any other carp bait. As the corn falls out of the spod it will drift down in the water and help to create a slightly wider patch of bait on the lake bed to bring many fish in from the surrounding area. The added colour in your spod mix will also be a massive help in bringing the carp in.

Specific Fishing Sweetcorn

Although sweetcorn from your local shop is great for carp fishing, there is a good selection of sweetcorn explicitly made for carp fishing. So are these just the same? No, not really. If you are willing to fork out a little extra for a tin, then these tins could add an extra edge to your carp fishing and help you get a few more fish on the banks. The corn in these tins is far larger than normal shop-bought sweet corn, making it a lot easier to get on a hair rig or hook. The bigger size may also encourage more fish to feed and help discourage the smaller nuisance fish in your swim. These specifically made tins will also have high sugar and salt content for added attraction in the water. Occasionally these tins will also have added flavourings such as tutti frutti or strawberry, which the carp just can't resist.

Imitation Corn

Another alternative to sweetcorn is imitation corn. This is just plastic pieces that are shaped the same as corn. This could seem counter-intuitive as we have already spoken about how the amino acid and sugar and salt content helps to bring in the surrounding fish. When using imitation corn it can be good practice to pair it with another bait such as a boilie or pellet and only use the corn to give the rig a slight edge.

This is entirely true, but imitation corn has its benefits;

- **Size** – Imitation corn comes in various sizes so you can choose a size depending on the fishing you are planning.
- **Weight** – Various weights are available with different buoyancy to balance your rig perfectly.
- **Flavour** – Although you won't get the usual salt, sugar and amino acid content in this corn you can buy it in added flavours.

Colouring and Flavouring Sweet Corn

If you don't fancy using any of these alternatives, you can still add to regular sweet corn to improve your carp fishing. By adding some simple food colouring, you can make your corn various colours. When sweet corn has been used to excess on some venues, the carp will stay well away from the yellow pieces to avoid getting caught.

Adding a squirt or two of flavouring to your shop-bought sweetcorn can also help to fool the fish into picking up your newly coloured and flavoured piece of corn.

Sweet corn is up there with the best baits for carp fishing and excels in many areas of carp fishing. I'm sure you can now see the benefits of taking sweetcorn to your next fishing session if you are looking to get some fish on the banks, no matter the time of year.

What are Boilies?

There are many baits that can be used to target carp. One of the best and most popular are boilies. Boilies are boiled baits that specifically go after carp. This presentation was developed in the U.K. to weed out the other types of fish and only target carp. So far, this is exactly what the boilies have accomplished, as not many other species will even bat an eye at a boilie.

Originally, boilies were super simple and could be made very easily. They still are relatively easy to make, but advancements in the industry have made the recipe a little more complicated. At its roots, a boilie is made of eggs and flour, preferably whole-wheat flour. Then, they will add some flavouring to really up the attractant qualities.

Then, the mixture is rolled into balls and hard-boiled. This cooks the inside while creating a skin-like exterior to add waterproofing features and some structural integrity. As you can see, these are super simple recipes that do a great job of delivering results. Ever since those early days of innovation, the boilie has evolved into a wide range of things. These presentations come in a variety of colours, sizes, materials, and attractants.

Boilies

The biggest carp fishing companies in the industry all have their paws in the boilie market. So, there is a wide variety of options that you can buy at your local carp fishing shop or online. You can also make them yourself as they did in the old days. This will save you some money and you will learn a new interesting skill.

Why Should you use Boilies?

It is all fine knowing what boilies are, but if you don't know when and why to use them, it is just background information that cannot be applied in the field. So, here we will lay out a few reasons why you should give boilies a try.

First off, boilies are very innovative and allow for a bit of creative freedom. Whether you choose to make them yourself or buy them from a manufacturer, the industry is constantly pushing the boundaries for what can be used in them. When fishing with sweetcorn, that is just about all you get. With boilies, there are colours, attractants, oils, and more that come with it.

Carp are brilliant fish. They want to eat what is healthy and nutritious to them. Believe it or not, the design, scent, and materials that makeup boilies are considered suitable for carp from their perspective. That is why they are so drawn to boilies. Over the years, commercial carp have come accustomed to relying on this type of bait to live.

Another really important factor to consider is the flavour of the boilie. Just like anything we eat, we have preferences for certain flavours. Carp are the same way. A couple of popular flavour profiles among the fish include sweet, fishy, natural, and sticky.

One of the most interesting is sweet. This is the same sweet flavour profile as we indulge in. Some popular flavours include Tutti Frutti, coconut, pineapple, strawberry, and many others. This is unique and probably the only presentation in all fishing that partially imitates something we would eat as humans.

Washing Out Boilies

One fantastic way to elevate your carp fishing game is by washing out your boilies. Washing them out is the act of fading the boilies with water. You simply soak the boilies in water for a few days and then use them.

This accomplishes a few different things. One of which is to fade the colour of the boilie. New boilies have pretty distinct colours and fresh appearances. Carp are more competent when we think. There are carp out there in overfished waters that see brand new boilies and just stay away because they know something is up. When the colour is far more faded and just sitting at the bottom, the carp will be more likely to trust it and take a bite.

Washing out the boilies also alter the chemical composition of the boilies. Different scenes and oils will be extracted to change the makeup. Again, if a carp is able to point out these distinct features, washing them out will trick them even more.

Another significant factor to consider is what the boilies are soaking up. When you throw a dry boilie into a pond, that boilie will quickly start to absorb up a lot of the features of that pond. If it is a little smelly and scummy, this will be reflected in the boilie. This isn't always bad but should be avoided in most cases.

When the boilies have already been soaked, there is a better likelihood that the pond's water won't disrupt the integrity of the boilie, at least not for a longer period of time. So, not only are you altering the boilies, you are making them stronger and able to last a lot longer.

To actually do the washing out, there are a few steps to keep in mind. Firstly, you need a bucket big enough to hold all of your boilies and the required amount of water. Then, you put the boilies in and put just enough water to cover them.

It is essential not to use tap water for this process. This is because tap water has certain chemicals in it that can throw off the composition. You should use clean lake water, bottled spring water, or boiled water.

Balancing Boilies

Finding the right balance for your presentation is significant. By balance, we mean using the correct size boilie for your rig and for the carp being targeted. This simple equation is vital to understand so you can take advantage of the materials at your disposal.

As you know by now, boilies come in varying sizes. These sizes can range to a small five millimetres in diameter to over 25. This is a huge difference. It would help if you did not pair a small hook with a 25-millimetre boilie. This is a recipe for disaster. On the flip side, you can't have a big hook connected with a five millimetre one. Either way, you are more than likely in for a day of no hook ups.

Along with your hook, you need to consider the size of fish you are targeting. In most cases, you probably will have a decent idea of how big the carp are in that specific area. As a general rule, when you know smaller carp will be targeted, use a boilie that is between 5 and 10 millimeters. When the carp start to get bigger, you can branch out into the 11-16 millimeter range. But, smaller boilies will still definitely catch larger carp.

Boilies or Pop-up Boilies?

Now that you know a bit more about boilies, it is time to introduce another way to present the bait. This is in the form of a pop-up. The regular boilie presentation simple rests on the bottom. Carp are bottom feeders and find comfort in sucking boilies up from the bottom. However, these aren't always the best presentations.

A pop-up boilie presentation allows the rig to sit slightly above the bottom of the waterway. The composition of the boilie is made to be more buoyant. The mix of the boilie is what makes it more buoyant. Companies use one tactic by mixing in cork dust, which holds air and elevates the bait in the water column.

Boilies

There are a few instances where having a boilie not sit on the bottom can be very helpful. Deciding to use a pop-up does require a little bit of field research and prior knowledge but nothing that you can't handle.

The biggest of which is when you know the bottom is filthy and silty. When there is no semi-solid bottom, the boilie can be lost in the muck and not visible to the carp. On that same note, a lot of pop-ups are brightly coloured so they can be seen amidst the filth. Colours like white and yellow are quite popular. .

Pellets are another great hook bait for carp that can see you into some nice fish. They may not be as widely used as the likes of boilles but that does not mean they should be discarded. Let's get into it.

What Are Pellets?

So, let's begin with the definitions, shall we? Alright. Well, a pellet is a modern food created to feed fish, made up of a mixture of vegetable proteins and binding agents (wheat) that has undergone extrusion. More elaborately, all the raw ingredients are forced through a small tube, which creates a sausage-like mix made harder by steam-cooking. Once done there, it's cut into smaller pieces so that you can use to catch carp and other fish species.

Other than vegetable matter, pellets contain fats, carbohydrates, minerals, and liquid/powdered additives. The raw ingredients of these substances include soybean cake, straw meal, and so forth. There are so many types of pellets ranging in size, texture, colour, and flavour. Don't know where to start? To make it easier for you, below are some pellet types. You can choose the one according to your preference.

Different Pellet Sizes

Pellets come in different sizes, and choosing the right one can be a bit difficult. But don't worry, I have gathered all the dimensions and their description here for you.

1mm Pellet

These tiny pellets are best to use in winter, where you don't want fish to gorge, as bites and feeding are scarce.

2mm Pellet

If you are using a method feeder, this Pellet is an excellent choice to feed fish in cold water. You need to make sure you're mixing these pellets to perfection , so they react optimally when your feeder and pellets hit the water. But, more on that later.

4mm Pellet

If you want a pellet that catches almost all manner of species, then this is the right size to pick. You can use it as a loose feed and it's also a good size for hookbait.

6mm Pellet

6mm pellets are also a good choice for catching varying sizes of fish. The slightly larger size helps to deter tiny nuisance fish. This won't stop them from pecking away and eventually knocking the pellet off your hook or hair rig. So, keep this in mind.

8mm Pellet

The 8mm pellet is a great size for many commercial carp baggers, and you can use a hair rig or band when using it. Again, it's best to catch bigger fish.

This list should make it easier for you to pick the right pellet size.

Texture

As strange as it might sound: yes, carp have a texture preference for pellets.

Experienced anglers say that a texture should mimic natural carp food such as worms. If it's soft, then fish will take time to chew it, and meanwhile, your hook can catch hold.

Isn't it getting stranger and stranger? Well, carp even fancy colourful food too. Let's learn a bit about different bait colours.

What Colour of Pellet to Use?

So, it turns out that some carp stick to a particular bait colour, whereas some choose their bait colour according to their surroundings. Pellet baits are available in multiple colours that vary from dull to bright. You can choose the one that best contrasts with your surroundings or is visible in murky water, for starters.

If you ask us to choose one, we'd prefer bright colours like pink, red, green, or yellow as they will grab carps attention. Try using yellow to resemble corn or food colour, which mimics the food that carp eat naturally. If you find it hard to select the correct colour, choosing flavour can be twice as hard as picking a colour. But we'll break it down for you quickly. The bottom line is all flavours and colours will catch fish but some might just give you the edge on certain days.

Choose the Right Flavour

The flavour is an essential tactic in carp fishing. Pellet bait comes in many varieties ranging from spicy, fishy, nutty, citrus, fruity to sweet. Carp's sense of smell and taste is powerful. They can sense their meal even in murky water. The local tackle shop will offer many other baits such as pop-ups and boilies. So, why would you choose pellets over other baits for carp fishing?

Why Should You Use Pellets?

Now an important question: why? If you've read everything until now, you must have some ideas as to why you should be trying pellets, but still, let's break it down further. Once a carp eats a pellet, it's hard for it to stop because of the pellet's protein content. Sometimes different recipes increase the nutritional value, and voila, the carp are addicted.

Other than "addiction", as we've already mentioned, pellets can be attractive because you can easily attract a carp from food appearance and taste. If you try fishing with Tutti Frutti flavour, chances are you will get an exceptional response because of its colour and flavour.

Plus, it comes in both high and low oil content you can pick according to the weather and fish type, which makes it a very personalised fishing experience, resulting in higher catches, if you get it just right.

Another advantage is that some pellets take longer to break down, and some break down easily. The pellet goes to the bottom of the water and starts dissolving in the water. The dissolved particles then send scent to carp, which they smell, and start following them to find the bait. Whether it be a pre-baited area or your hook bait.

Pellets

Hence, this helps in catching carp. But there are different varieties of pellets in the market, which works best for you will depend on the tactic you wish to perform and the fishing venue.

Types of Pellets

All baits are not created equally. Some types of baits are low in oil content, some take longer to break down, and others are great for adding to a hair rig. Let's look at different pellet types.

Trout Pellets

Carp loves these pellets as they comprise salmon fry crumb and are rich in protein and oil, therefore best to use in summer. Why in summer? Oil will disperse better in the warmer water.

Halibut Pellets

Halibut pellets are high in oil content, nutrients, and proteins. These pellets are good at creating free bait beds and are often drilled in bigger sizes for use on hair rigs. If you want to catch big carp, chub, and specimen bream, then you should try these.

Hemp Pellets

Only a few fresh-water fish don't like them, but they are still excellent carp and tench attractors. These pellets break down into mush and work well in groundbait mixes and PVA bags. You can also use them as loose feed. You can use them effectively throughout the year.

Carp Pellets

If there's a ban on trout and halibut in your area because of their high oil, you can use carp pellets. These pellets contain vegetable proteins, low oil and break down quickly. Carp pellets are best used as loose feed and not as hook bait.

Corn Steep Liquor Pellets

CSL pellet breakdown rapidly in water and forms a fine bed of attractive particles. You can also use these as loose feeds and in method mixes or PVA bags. Many species, particularly barbel and carp, love them.

Soft Pellets

These pellets contain moisture and are small, making them ideal for carp and silverfish. These are soft and available in sizes ranging from 1mm to 4mm. You can use them directly on the hook or hair rig them. These pellets are also used for method feeder mix.

Shapes of Pellets

When fishing for larger fish, you can use regular pellets as loose feed or hook bait pellets ranging from 6mm to 20mm. It's hard to get a hook through these pellets as they are hard. However, you can get around this by using various methods:

Banded Pellets

You can use a bait band on your rigs to put around these pellets to keep them on your rig. Another method is to drill your pellet; this takes extra time and effort but is more likely to stay on your rig.

Pellets

Drilled Pellets

Another great way to present a pellet hookbait is to put it on a hair rig. For this method, you need a baiting needle, and some hair stops. Pre-tied hair rigs will also work just fine for this. These pellets will be pre-drilled so you can easily put the pellet onto your rig.

Expander Pellets

These pellets remain in shape for a long time and are ideal for directly adding to hook bait. You can add these hard pellets to water to soften and create a spongy texture. Expander pellets are floating pellets, but after soaking, they sink because of hook weight.

Sometimes, some simple methods work better than anything else that you've tried. That may be the case when it comes to carp fishing with bread. If you're looking for a simple yet effective bait, it is time for you to explore fluffier alternatives like plain old white bread!

Corn, boilies and pellets are indeed great baits to use when carp fishing. But what should you use when you want to switch up your bait but don't want to go for anything too complicated? Use bread, of course!

Bread may seem like an uninspiring choice to beginners. However, there's a reason why so many experienced anglers swear by it. Bread is one of the most effective baits for when you go on a carp fishing expedition. If used correctly, it'll help you reel in quite a few carp. But what makes bread so great as bait? Let's find out.

It is Economical

It doesn't matter where you live. Bread is always an extremely cheap option for bait. Many anglers use it to catch carp without spending money on expensive boilies combined with its effectiveness. Fishing gear and baits can get very expensive. If you don't have a lot of money to burn, you can save by using bread as bait.

Bread

It is Readily Available

Is your fishing expedition all planned out but you've forgot to buy bait? You have no reason to worry. Just get yourself a loaf of bread, and you're good to go. If you're going for the simplest bread bait, just stick some rolled-up bread onto a size eight circle hook. While it may not stay hooked for very long, it'll still help you attract carp to the general area and give you a chance at hooking into one.

It is Highly Visible

The bright white colour of bread is one of the reasons that make it an excellent bait. Anglers typically find carp in murky, shadowy waters. In such waters, visibility is low, so the bait will need to be a colour they can easily spot. Carp can easily see white baits even in darker surroundings because it tends to stand out.

Excellent Bait for Surface Fishing

Surface fishing is a great technique to catch carp in the summer months. Just attach the bread bait directly to your hook if you're not going to cast it very far away. However, ensure that your line isn't too visible. A visible line can spook away the fish as carp are well-known for rejecting bait that looks dangerous.

Carp Adore Bread

Now that's something you probably didn't know. Much like ducks, fish such as carp are also huge fans of bread. Their sharp sense of smell and eyesight helps them zero in on the bread pieces. So, if you're having a slow day on the water, just toss a few bread balls into the water to spice things up a bit and see if you can attract any hungry carp to the surface.

Easily Customisable

Want softer textures? Use soaked bread. Want compact balls as bait? Add some breadcrumbs to the soaked bread mixture. There are various ways to customise your bread bait according to the water, the fish, and the season. For instance, to improve visibility even more, you can add bright colours to the mixture. Add some liquid flavours to the bread mixture to aid the carp's smell to make a bait that the fish simply cannot resist.

Fishing With Bread On The Surface

Surface fishing is prevalent among anglers in the summer months. This popularity comes from the fact that, depending on the circumstances, surface fishing can be a very easy or complicated technique to succeed with.

However, if you see carp swimming close to the surface from where you stand, you can hook your bread balls directly to the hook and cast them. The great thing about using bread as bait is that its lightweight causes it to land calmly on the water's surface.

This calm landing doesn't scare the fish away as boilies or pellets do sometimes do. While surface fishing, you can use this to your advantage by casting the bread close to where you see the fish swimming. The fish will come closer to investigate or even take the floating bread.

Take care to ensure that while surface fishing, fishing equipment, and clothing are not very prominent, which can scare away the fish. You should also remember that you will need to add some weighted assistance to your hook if you plan on casting your bread bait a little farther away. Bread is extremely light, and it will struggle to strip line from your reel.

Bread

Using Bread For Baiting Swims

Another great thing about bread, as discussed above, is its versatility. Whether you use it as bread balls, after running it through a food processor, or after loading it in a spod or a spomb, you get great results each time. So, what are some methods for baiting swims with bread? Let's see.

Spod or Spomb

There are two ways to go about this. You can load these up with plain bread crumbs to create an attractive cloud of bait for carp to come closer to, or you can make a spod mix with bread as an ingredient. To make a spod mix, all you need to do is fire up your food processor and mash-up your bread into a fine mixture. Then add some different ingredients according to your liking. These ingredients can be anything from condensed milk, corn, and hempseeds to crushed pellets. Mix these in a tub, then let it sit for a little while. After that, load up your spod or spomb with the mixture for a bait that you can cast off into quite the distance.

PVA bags

PVA bags are growing in popularity among anglers because of their easy usage and great results. So, how can you incorporate bread into the mix? You can liquidise your bread in a food processor and add some additives such as maggots, crushed pellets, or liquidised boilies to it. Load up in a PVA bag, and you've found a great way to utilise your bread. Add some colouring if you want to add a little more attraction to your PVA bread bags.

Bread Pack Bait

Bread is also a great ingredient in pack baits which is a lot more prominent across the pond in the US. A basic recipe for a pack bait includes:

- Blended bread.
- Some jelly mix in your choice's flavour.
- A firming ingredient such as wheat bran.

Some other ingredients that you can include bird seeds or crushed pellets. The methods mentioned above should give you an idea about how you can bait your swims with bread.

Using Bread For Fishing At The Bottom

Whether surface fishing or fishing at the bottom, bread emerges as excellent bait for all carp fishing techniques. Why is that? It is because bread is something that anglers can process in a hundred different ways to get the results they want.

So, how can you hook some bottom-feeding carp with the help of bread? Let's find out. Anglers can fish bread balls in much the same way as boilies. All you need to do is roll the bread into small, round balls. If you feel like the balls are too loose, you can also add a firming mixture such as brown bread crumbs. This addition helps them stay on more firmly. Bread balls initially float when you cast them. They gradually absorb water, get heavier, and rest near the bottom, where carp are scavenging for food.

When To Use Bread

A good angler judges which bait to use according to the water, the weather, and the fish they wish to catch. Bread is also a suitable bait in certain circumstances. So, which are they? Let's discuss them.

Fish Close to the Surface

Surface fishing is very effective with bread as bait. Just cast your bait close by and wait for the carp to come close to the delicious bread waiting for them.

When the Carp Need a Change of Pace

In commercial fisheries and busy spots like that, it is essential to switch up your bait once in a while. This change of pace is necessary because fish can judge a bait as dangerous if cast repeatedly in the same spot. Since most anglers do not use bread very often, it is an excellent idea for fishing trips where the carp do not seem interested in standard baits such as boilies or corn.

When Not To Use Bread

Like all baits, there are instances when bread isn't such a good idea. An experienced angler does not rely on just one bait for all conditions. It is essential to know when carp fishing with bread may not be as successful as other conditions. So, when does bread make a poor choice of bait? Let's see.

When the Water has a Duck or Goose Population

We all know ducks and geese love bread. It is impossible to bait the fish in areas where people feed the waterfowl without attracting a flock of those birds. These birds cause such a disturbance that the carp get spooked and move away. The waterfowl also eat the bread bait.

In Places Where Using White Bread is Banned

Some UK places have banned anglers from using white bread as bait, which is considered unhealthy for the carp. It is essential to respect the rules and use other baits in place of white bread in places like these. Well, that's all on where you shouldn't use bread as bait.

What Bread To Use In Each Scenario

If we've convinced you that bread is an excellent idea for carp fishing, you need to know which bread works best in which circumstances. Some things to remember when using bread as bait are:

- Breadcrumbs are good firming ingredients. Anglers can use them to pack baits, fill PVA bags with, and fill up spods or spombs.
- For surface fishing, use bread balls with some crust in them as the crust is durable and helps the bait stay afloat for longer without breaking apart.
- White bread is a suitable bait for almost all conditions.
- Brown bread is a good alternative in places where white bread is banned.

Carp fishing with bread is gratifying when done right. An angler needs to know everything there is to know about the various types of baits they can make with bread and all the conditions they can use that bait to be successful at catching carp.

So, if you've learned any useful tricks from this section, it's time to give carp fishing with bread a try!

Carp fishing with maggots can work exceptionally well for catching carp, especially in the colder winter months. In these colder months, the carp become less active; they feed less and move less. When they feed, it's usually a smaller amount than in the warm months and they are much more selective; this is part of why maggots are so effective during this time. Let's dive into some tips and tactics for carp fishing with maggots.

When to Use Maggots

Maggots are primarily used in the winter months when fishing for carp can be exceptionally tough. During these months, the maggot bite will usually get good, typically from December to March. During this period of famine in terms of bites, maggots can be the key to enticing the carp out of their lethargic state. If done correctly, they can even outperform your summer fishing action when you fish an effective swim due to the fish keying in on natural food sources and not other types of presentations.

Maggot Fishing Tactics

When arriving at your fishing spot, be prepared to spod or throw about a gallon of maggots. You want your bait bed to be reasonably small, but a little spread is preferred; this is why I would recommend a spod over say PVA bags. The great thing about maggots is that they wriggle around and spread a bit on their own. Carp actively feeding on your bed of maggots will waft them around while feeding with the vacuum like mouths and tail action.

This spreads the maggots out, and keeps them there for hours, even overnight. This spreading action keeps carp in the swim that you're fishing for hours as they attempt to root out every single last maggot.

Nuisance Fish

Many carp anglers avoid using maggots because of nuisance fish such as bream, tench and silver fish eating their bait. But in the winter months, bream and tench live by the same rules as carp, with slower feeding habits in the cold water. Nuisance fish eat much less than carp during this time, and in the winter months, it isn't usually a problem. With only minor exceptions, you might only catch one of these fish here or there, but it is by far a constant issue.

Keep Rigging simple

Keeping your rigs simple is probably your best bet here; we are looking for small, natural, and subtle presentations. In most cases, you can even scratch the need for threading with needles and bait links and put 6 or so maggots directly on your hook. Maggots are going to wriggle around on the hook and give an incredibly appealing presentation.

Caring for Your Maggots
Storage

The best place to store maggots when you are not fishing is in the fridge (wife's or families approval recommended), this can keep your maggots alive and happy for up to two weeks. The cold of the fridge slows their metabolism down enough to prevent them from turning into casters. Oh, by the way, always keep a lid on them to avoid damp maggots from venturing into your wife's casserole if she agrees to allow you to keep maggots in the fridge. If you don't have the ability to keep maggots in your fridge, keep them someplace that's dark and cool, the garage, or better yet, in a bait box floating in a bucket or tub of water.

Maggots

Bring out the dead

Be sure when you have stored your bait somewhere that will allow them to survive for weeks, that you go and pick out any maggots that have turned into casters or died. This will keep the rest from the same fate more quickly than normal.

Riddle me this

One great way to separate large quantities of living maggots from dead ones is to use a riddle. Grab yourself a bucket and a riddle and put the riddle over the bucket and add all your maggots. The living maggots will wriggle their way through the riddle, leaving all debris and dead maggots in the riddle itself.

Now, our next tip is a very important one in regards to your wife. As a consolation prize, you can give the dead maggots to your wife! She can use them to feed the birds out in the garden, her favourite birds will happily munch on the dead maggots.

The Path Less Travelled

As mentioned, many carp anglers shy away from maggots due to them thinking that the nuisance fish makes it not worth the time and effort. We also explained how in the winter months when maggots are truly effective that this issue isn't much of, well, an issue. On pressured bodies of water maggots can really outshine everything due to not being used much.

And likewise, once you start doing well with maggots on a body of water, I would even encourage you to bring your friends there and have them throw maggots in multiple areas. This will tune in the carp to feed on them regularly after feeding on your large baitings of free maggots from spodding, and over time can actually make maggots the best big carp catching bait you can throw on that body of water.

Maggots

Pros and Cons of Maggot Fishing

Pros

- Can be devastating in the winter months to big carp
- Simple rigging is all that's needed
- Last a decent amount of time in between fishing sessions

Cons

- Requires some daily maintenance during storage to keep alive
- Can attract nuisance fish to your bait offerings
- Wife might have reservations about keeping a colony of creepy crawlies in the fridge

Carp fishing with maggots is something that you should not shy away from, particularly in the winter months. Many carp anglers shy away from these presentations, but let's be honest, to an opportunistic angler, you should embrace that mentality and exploit it. The lack of anglers fishing with maggots means that the fish see them less frequently and are more prone to accept your offering.

Rigs

Rigs

You're probably wondering by now — when do we learn about the rigs? Here it is! Rigs are an essential part of your carp fishing setup. A fishing rig generally refers to how you tie a certain piece of tackle to your fishing line. Most fishing methods use specific fishing rigs to catch certain types of fish in certain situations. This section will tell you all there is to know about the different types of fishing rigs.

Method Feeder

This rig is a fairly popular one among carp anglers, so it makes sense that we start with this. So, what is the method feeder, what is it used for, and how can you master the technique yourself?

Rig Description

Anglers struggle with presenting their bait so that the carp aren't suspicious of it. The method feeder is a brilliant way to present your hookbait so that the fish are less suspicious of your rig and won't question picking up your hookbait.

The method feeder is a small plastic object that allows anglers to neatly deliver their bait to the bottom, where the carp will devour it. The feeder comes with a mould that helps you shape your bait mix around your method feeder. Both your hook bait and hook lie buried within the mound of bait mix that's moulded around your method feeder. The method feeder is weighted to always land on its bottom while presenting the mountain of bait on top. When the carp see the mountain of bait lying at the lake bottom, they get attracted to it without even spotting the hook.

Best Situations For The Rig

Most anglers will tell you that the method feeder is an evergreen rig that is useful for all kinds of fishing venues and seasons. Whether you are an amateur or a pro, one of the simplest and most fun ways to reel in some mighty carp is to try the method feeder.

However, many anglers love using method feeders to catch carp in the winter. As you may know, carp typically hibernate or slow down on feeding in the winters, which can cause you to have some very boring fishing trips. Carp typically gather in any one area of the lake, and you just need to find that sweet spot to get the action going. For that reason, it's important to cast around until you register a line bite or even catch a carp. Most anglers use method feeders in the winters, so they distribute adequate bait at the bottom for any fish to find. In any case, it's important to remember that method feeder fishing is not just useful for fishing in the winters. You can use it year-round for a neat bottom presentation and some great catches.

Pros and Cons of Method Feeder Fishing

As a beginner, you should try out every carp rig at least once, regardless of its pros and cons, to gain some experience in how the carp react to different rigs. Doing so will allow you to learn which rig is best suited for which situation and so on.

There are quite a few pros of method feeder fishing that one can talk about. Firstly, it's one of the most convenient ways to deliver a nice mountain of bait to the bottom where the carp can feast on it. It's also great for loading and reloading quickly when you need to bait a wide area of the lake. You should also use it for fishing over slopes or shelves because the flat bottom of the method feeder will allow your bait to neatly present over gradually sloping areas where it might be hard for other rigs to do so. You should also use the method feeder when you encounter a lot of suspicious carp.

Since a lot of anglers have switched to PVA bags now, the method feeder might be a good change of pace for the lake's inhabitants. Another benefit of this rig is that you can switch up your bait mix according to the carp's preferences. Add some liquid attractants to the bait to make it tastier, and switch between groundbait, breadcrumbs and micropellets to get the perfect mix for your lake's hungry carp. Another great selling point for the method feeder is that there's very little chance of it tangling in vegetation or debris when you cast close to islands or the bank if you use a short hook link.

One of the cons of method feeders as rigs in well-populated lakes is their appeal to nuisance fish. Sometimes, the nuisance fish will slurp the contents of the feeder and give you a false alarm long before any carp shows up. This rig is also not as aerodynamic as other ones, so you might have trouble casting over large distances accurately. So, if you're doing some ambitious casting over long distances, method feeders might not be it.

Other Feeders

While method feeders are the most popular feeder types, a few others work on the same philosophy but have different bodies and, ultimately, different uses.

Open-Ended Feeder

Open-ended feeders are used less than method feeders, but you'll probably still see them from time to time.

Rig Description

As their name indicates, open-ended feeders are open on both sides. However, they are less exposed than method and cage feeders, so a lot less bait escapes as it goes down in the water. Much like the method feeder, it's an excellent tool for delivering bait to the bottom of the lake where the carp will find it.

Best Situations For The Rig

Open-ended feeders are typically well-suited to fishing in deep waters. If you pack it really well, the bait won't leak out before it hits the bottom, where it'll create an appetising cloud for the nearby carp. In addition, it's also great for when you're baiting the swim with fine particles such as breadcrumbs because they have a hard time escaping from the open-ended feeder on the way down. Many anglers use open-ended feeders when nuisance fish are hanging around the swim. Since the open-ended feeder releases almost no cloud of bait on its way down, there's a chance that the nuisance fish won't follow its scent and devour it before the carp have a chance to.

Pros And Cons Of Open-Ended Feeder

There are a few things that the open-ended feeder is great for. One of these things is securely depositing the bait on the lake bed. You'll see that the closed walls of the feeder are great for baiting deep swims or those with flowing water. Although a lot of us rarely fish in flowing water in the UK for carp, it's still a good option to keep in mind for when you do. In addition, you can deposit fine bait such as breadcrumbs, maggots and chopped worms safely to the bottom by filling the feeder's centre with the fine bait and plugging the sides with groundbait. Doing so will secure the bait, and you won't have a cloud going all the way down, which might make the nuisance species chase it down. If you're fishing over a steep shelf, an open-ended plastic feeder will be very helpful because it will rise earlier, easily helping you overcome the obstacle.

However, if you want to release the bait quickly, the open-ended feeders are not the thing for you. If the fishing you have in mind requires you to release a tasty cloud down the swim, you'll need to opt for a cage feeder instead of an open-ended one.

Cage Feeder

As its name indicates, the cage feeder is a feeder that has holes all around it, making it look like a cage. It's a very handy piece of tackle for a lot of reasons.

Rig Description

The cage feeder is made to look like a cage to allow rapid release of its contents into the swim. This type of rig is excellent for attracting the nearby carp to your bait because all the holes will make sure that your bait gets flushed out as it descends the water.

Best Situations For The Rig

This rig is typically used where depth isn't your priority. Since this feeder has a lot of holes on all sides, it's great for baiting shallow swims where you need an attractive cloud of bait to attract the carp. If you're fishing in a swim with low visibility, you might like to use cage feeders, and we'll discuss why in the pros and cons section.

Pros And Cons

The one thing anglers are always waxing poetic about when it comes to the cage feeder is that it's easy to load and unload. This quality gives your fishing a lot of speed which is critical most times when the carp are busy feeding, and you want to be in the thick of the action. In addition, if you're doing close-range fishing at shallow depths, the cage feeder will be your best bet to disperse your bait quickly. Another great thing about the cage feeder is that if the visibility in the water is low, you can load it with brightly-coloured corn, which will give you quite an edge on an otherwise dull day. The carp will be able to make out the bright colours of the corn even in murky waters and hopefully end up biting.

The cons are few, but they are there. The most obvious demerit of the cage feeder is that you absolutely cannot use it to bait deep swims because the cage feeder will be empty by the time it hits the bottom. You also cannot trust its accuracy much when there's a wind blowing because of its side-weighted quality. This side-weighted quality also means that you cannot cast them over long distances. These days, manufacturers have come up with bottom-weighted feeders which do not have these problems.

Maggot Feeder

The maggot feeder is our last instalment of the feeder fishing rigs. As its name indicates, you use it to bait the swim with live maggots, the oldest and most trustworthy baits on the market today.

Rig Description

Since maggots are hard to bait without directly hooking them on, anglers use the maggot feeder to bait the swim with large quantities of maggots. The maggot feeder is a hollow plastic or metal tube with a few big holes in it through which the maggots wriggle out.

Best Situations For The Rig

If you ask us, we'll say that the maggot is a bait that fails to get old, much like corn. You can fish this anywhere at any time and see great results. However, it's better to fish it at the end of winter or the start of spring when the carp haven't started actively feeding yet. These pockets of sleepy carp will only venture out of their respective groups if they see something that smells and looks good, such as a maggot. With a maggot feeder, you can bait the swim with as many maggots as you want!

Pros And Cons

One of the pros of the maggot feeder is that it works like a slow-release bait. The maggots will slowly wriggle out of the feeder, giving the carp a continuous supply of bait to munch on, after which one of them will ultimately take the hookbait. Another great quality of maggot feeders is that you can add some liquid and powder attracts to the maggots and then load the feeder with them, which can give your bait the extra kick it needs. You can also fit a lot of maggots in a feeder, so you'll be able to bait the swim quite a bit, even in one go.

One of the main cons of the maggot feeder is that you cannot fish it over long distances with accuracy. In addition, you'll need to load and reload the feeder quite a few times to bait the swim fully, but it takes a bit of time to load the feeder each time because the maggots keep wriggling out. You'll also need to pack in a lot of maggots in one feeder to adequately bait your swim, which will take time because of their continuous movement. The feeder also empties slowly on the bottom of the lake, so if you had a quick recasting in mind, remember that you can't do it with a maggot feeder.

PVA Bag Rig

The PVA bag rig is one of the most popular angling setups that you'll see on your fishing trips. It's terrific for attracting a lot of hungry carp because the PVA bags serve as little bags filled with delicious goodies that are slowly released into the lake bed. It's one of the most effective fishing techniques for carp fishing so pay attention to this one!

Rig Description

A PVA bag is a small water-soluble plastic bag that you can fill with micropellets, groundbait, or any other bait mix along with the hookbait. When you fish this bag on a PVA bag rig, it starts breaking up in the water, slowly releasing its contents to the lake bed, where the hungry carp will gulp it up. Doing so will cause them to come across your hookbait presented within. This rig draws comparisons to feeder fishing because it also neatly presents the hookbait on or in a small mountain of bait.

Best Situations For The Rig

This versatile rig is generally well-suited to nearly all carp fishing situations. However, there are some instances in which the PVA bag shines, so let's discuss what those are. First off, PVA bags are your best friends when you need to cast in a far-off spot. Their tight packing and aerodynamic design give it a lot of momentum to fly off to the other side of the bank. So, if you see some carp breaking the surface on the opposite side of the lake, you might want to fill up a PVA bag or two. Secondly, it's great for fishing at the very bottom of the lake, much like method feeders. Since the PVA bag sinks to the bottom every time, it's an excellent tool for carp fishing because the carp are bottom-feeders and love finding treats on the lake bed.

A lot of anglers love using PVA bags in the winter. This preference stems from the fact that the carp don't eat a lot in the winters, so they need something special to get them to feed. This rig will make them come out of their slumber and let the anglers have some fun. Another situation in which the PVA bag might shine is when you're fishing in the weeds. While dense weeds might be problematic, the carp love finding a mound of goodies in some light weed growths. You can also fish it in slightly silty lake beds because it won't get completely buried in the depth of the silt. There is a big difference between light fishable weed and dense weed fishing with a PVA bag so keep this in mind.

Pros And Cons Of PVA Bag Rigs

PVA bag rigs are one of the most widely used rigs in every lake, and there's a good reason for that. It has quite a long list of pros, which we are now going to discuss. One thing that makes PVA bags a great choice is that they work in nearly every swim. If you're fishing in a new place and don't quite know its secrets yet, fish it with a PVA bag to get great results.

The great thing about PVA bags is also that you fish the hookbait with the tasty offerings to bring in the carp and keep them there, so there's a greater chance of a bite. When you're spodding or spombing, even a little casting inaccuracy can result in a failed endeavour. PVA bags are also quite aerodynamic when you pack them well and turn in their corners, so if you're looking for a rig to fish over long distances, this one is it. Many anglers also prefer this rig for winter fishing. The reason behind this preference is that the carp don't feed heavily in winter, so a lot of bait won't do much in attracting them. However, a small concentration of tasty treats might make them come closer, resulting in a few bites in the offseason as well.

While it is a great rig all over, it has a few cons as well. The first one is its water solubility. That solubility is a great weapon in the water. Outside of it? Not so much. These bags dissolve when they come in contact with anything that's water-based, such as sweaty hands, a spot of rain, condensation from a cold bottle, etc. Since a lot of anglers enjoy fishing on rainy days, PVA bags become a little bit of a problem. Another reason why you might struggle with using PVA bags is that it's a little time-consuming when you want to recast.

However, a lot of anglers get around that by filling their PVA bags before they start fishing and storing them in a waterproof bag until it's time to use them. Another problem with this rig is that you cannot use liquid attractants with it since any water-based ingredient will cause the PVA bags to dissolve. Since most anglers love to spice up their bait mixes with these attractants, it's hard to fish without them.

Chod Rig

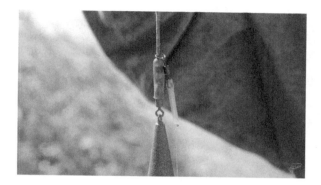

Chod rig is another economical yet versatile option for anglers in the UK. You'll hear most anglers mention it when they're discussing fishing in weed cover, and you're about to find out why it is the magic cure to choddy waters (choddy water are waters that have debris or weed covered bottoms).

Rig Description

If you fish any regular rig in choddy waters, it's either going to get unbelievably tangled, or the line is going to break. If neither of these things happens, you still won't get a bite because the weedy growths obscure the bait from view, and no fish sees it. The presentation is awful when fishing over weeds, but the chod rig makes it much easier to do that.

This rig has a lead attached to it that sinks to the bottom as soon as you fish it. The hookbait will slide up the line with the buoyancy of the pop-up attached to it. Since this rig will present the hookbait perfectly over the weeds, the fish will find it quite interesting, and you'll definitely get a few bites with this method if there is fish in the area taking cover in the weeds.

Best Situations For The Rig

As is obvious from the name, the main use of this rig is to fish it over choddy waters. Chod is another name for the weed or silt one finds at the bottom of the lake. A newbie angler might ask, why is it so important to fish over chod? The answer to that is — because that's where a lot of carp can be! Carp love to seek cover, especially when the season is in full swing. So, if you see a rocky outcropping, an island, the shade from overhanging branches, some underwater debris or a dense weedy growth, there's a guarantee that you'll find carp there. So, if you're at a very busy lake and having no luck, try fishing the chod rig over some weeds.

It's also a great option for when you don't know what the bottom is like. Since this rig works great in all situations, you can fish it even when the swim isn't weedy and get great results. You should definitely give this rig a try when you've pre-baited a spot with the help of spods or spombs or even the good ol' throwing stick.

Pros And Cons Of Chod Rigs

There are quite a few pros of chod rigs. One of the main ones, as mentioned earlier, is that you don't really need to know what the bottom is like before fishing it with a chod rig. This tip is especially great for whenever the visibility is really low such as in murky waters or on an overcast day. You should also opt for a chod rig when you're short on money and don't want to spend too much on groundbait, micropellets and PVA bags. Another great thing about this rig is that it's almost too easy to get bites with this setup. However, you do need to know how to set it up properly.

One of the main cons is that it can get buried if you use it for fishing very thick weeds. It is up to the angler to make the distinction between manageable weeds and weeds that will cause their chod rig to get stuck in them. In addition, since the whole idea of chod rigs is based on buoyant pop-ups, you can't really use bottom baits or wafters with this kind of rig.

Ronnie Rig

The Ronnie Rig is a relative newcomer in the angling world, but it's one of the most effective rigs out there. It's similar to the chod rig in its action, but it is presented much closer to the bottom than the chod rig.

Rig Description

This rig is basically a pop-up rig. You tie it by attaching a long curved hook with something like a pop-up boilie secured with a hook rig stop. This arrangement allows the rig to present the boilie in waters that may be slightly populated with weeds and debris. It acts like a claw that hooks deeply into the mouth of the fish and makes sure you lose less fish after the hook is set.

Best Situations For The Rig

This rig presents the pop-up boilie slightly above the lake bed, making it an excellent choice for fishing in slightly choddy waters. If the weeds and the silt aren't too deep at all, your bait will be in the perfect position to be snapped up by a hungry carp passing by. This arrangement also ensures that the line doesn't get tangled and resets itself when it does, making it a great choice for swims populated by nuisance fish and birds. It's also great for when you know the swim is populated by wary carp that fight hard. Their struggles are less likely to result in an unhooking because of the swivel the rig is mounted on.

Most anglers will tell you that you can use this versatile rig anywhere you like as long as the water isn't too choddy. The Ronnie rig is your best bet to hook in some powerful carp in spots with light weeds, gravel, silt, and showing fish. It's also a favourite among anglers trying some winter fishing. We always say that you can't win over the carp in the winters with a whole lot of bait. However, fishing the swim with a single, bright-coloured bait with high attraction can definitely result in a bite, even in the dead of winter. It's even better because you can fish this rig near the bottom of the lake, which is popular among fish in the winters.

Pros And Cons Of The Ronnie Rig

It feels like this rig appeared out of nowhere and took over the carp fishing scene, but its popularity stems from its numerous advantages. One such advantage is that you can use it with quite possibly any hook you like, which is something you can't do with other rigs that have hooks with swivels attached, such as the 360s rig. Not only that, but it's also a great option to fish on venues where the use of the 360s rig is banned. This rig has nearly the same action but without the lateral movement that the 360s was popular for. It's also an excellent choice because of how impervious it is to the movements of nuisance fish species.

It's very useful for attracting carp cruising the bottom while scavenging for food. However, this action makes it nearly useless for fishing near the surface. There aren't many cons to this rig except that you might struggle with tying it in the start. However, that holds true for nearly all rigs and is something that definitely gets much better with constant practice!

Carp Care

Carp Care

How Long can carp Survive out of Water

This is a common question many anglers may have asked themselves, in particular new anglers. There isn't a definite answer, and many things can come into play about how long carp can survive out of water. Still, the important thing is to limit the time any fish you intend to release spends out of the water and that the proper steps are taken to ensure a safe release.

Carp and Oxygen

Carp are very tough fish, and studies have shown this in detail. Researchers have found that carp can live in environments with critically low oxygen levels for long periods. Depending on the oxygen levels available, they can survive in environments with low oxygen levels for days or even months.

Researchers have found that carp can change the structure of its gills to avoid becoming anoxic. Its blood has a high level of affinity for oxygen, more so than any other vertebrate. It even can produce a tranquiliser-type chemical and produce alcohols to help it survive when oxygen levels are deficient. But the time in which a carp can survive in these conditions depends on multiple factors, with the water temperature being a critical component.

We have heard that the Dutch used to catch carp and wrap them in wet or damp blankets and keep them in the cellar for days prior to eating, but just because carp can live for days in such a state doesn't mean that we should subject them to anything but the smallest amount of time possible outside of water for their well-being.

Carp Care

Critical Carp Care

As carp anglers, we honestly shouldn't even wonder the question of how long carp can survive out of the water, but rather focus on keeping any carp out of the water for the shortest amount of time possible. Even if they can survive in low oxygen environments, removing them from the water does more than stifle their oxygen intake.

Fish have slime coatings that protect them from harmful things like bacteria and infection if injured. When you remove a carp from the water, you can remove this part of this protective coating, making them susceptible to infections and harmful bacteria. This is why making sure your hands are wet when handling a fish and using the proper tools is important. Carp are also susceptible to gill damage if they are out of water for too long due to the gills drying out or getting covered in debris like dirt, so it is critical to limit the time out of water.

Cold weather can also be very harmful to carp, especially if the temperatures are well below freezing. Taking any fish out of the water in these conditions may allow the water on the gills and eyes to freeze and crystalise, and this will cause severe damage to the fish if they are in this situation, even for what may seem to be short amounts of time.

Proper Carp Handling Tools

In order to handle carp in the best way possible, you are going to want to have the correct tools for the job. In modern carp angling, there are many tools on the market to aid in the process of a successful release.

Carp Care

Mats

Unhooking mats are an essential release tool for carp anglers. When a fish is caught and landed on shore, you simply lay the fish down on the mat to unhook it with the least amount of damage possible. Just be sure to wet the mat before you use it or risk potential harm to the fish by removing its protective slime coating.

Large Landing Nets

Landing nets are also crucial in safely catching and releasing carp. Without a landing net, you have to drag the carp onto the bank, risking potential bodily harm to the fish and, without a doubt removing the slime coat. You can scoop up the fish and quickly transfer it to a damp unhooking mat with a landing net.

Be sure when you carry the fish from the water to the mat in a net that you leave your reel open to provide a slack line and that you aren't putting tension on the line as this could pull on the hook and damage the carps mouth.

Pliers and Forceps

When removing a hook from a carps mouth, pliers and forceps are a must-have. These tools allow you to pop out a hook with minimal damage quickly, and it doesn't hurt to have some long-jawed forceps and pliers to get hooks that are embedded deeper in a carp's mouth.

If a carp has the hook incredibly deep and unreachable by any tool and if it can't be done in a safe manner without causing severe harm to the fish, your best option is to cut your line as close to the hook as possible, while the hook will remain in the fish, over time the hook will rust or corrode and come out, this is the best chance for the survival of the fish.

In the United States, this practice is common among anglers, especially bass anglers. If a bass gets stomach hooked after rapidly eating a bait, the anglers will cut either the hook shank or the line and release it, as removal could cause severe damage and potentially kill the fish from blood loss.

Cameras and Tripod

While this might not seem like a release tool, it is still important. Having a camera and tripod that is set up and ready to snap a picture at the push of a button greatly aids in limiting the time that a carp spends out of water. Once the fish is on the mat and the hook removed, all you have to do is turn the camera on, and push a button with a delay timer, lift the fish up, snap a photo, and back into the drink it goes!

Releasing Carp

When you release a carp, you need to be sure that it's successful. This obviously means not simply throwing the fish in the water and calling it a day. Cradle or support the fish under its belly, and hold onto the tailstock of the fish, and let it rest in the water for as long as it needs to. The fish will tell you when it's ready to go back home and will attempt to kick away, and you will feel its tail tense up. This means you should loosen your grip and let the fish simply swim out of your hands.

If the rumours are to be believed in the right conditions, even a wet blanket and a damp cellar could keep carp alive for a surprising amount of time, and we know from research that carp can live in environments that other fish simply couldn't.

This doesn't mean carp anglers should be lax on the amount of time that a carp spends out of the water, and we should still strive to use the proper catch and release techniques to ensure it has the best chances for survival.

How to Hold Carp

How you hold your catch on the bank is essential to get a decent looking picture and ensure the carp is not injured and stress levels are kept to a minimum. Thankfully the process of holding a carp properly is relatively easy, all you'll need to do is follow a few simple steps to lift the fish correctly, take a good picture and return the carp to the water with as little stress as possible.

This book has a strong focus on how to catch carp but how you handle the carp when it's out the water is also essential. This section will focus solely on how to hold carp with step-by-step instructions: you really can't go wrong.

Why is it important to hold carp correctly?

Holding a fish correctly is not only required to take great pictures but it is also essential to keep the carp as comfortable as possible when outside of the water. Any damage caused to the fish reduces the quality of the fish and can even result in the carp dying if you are not briefed on how you should handle the fish.

As carp anglers it is our concern to make sure the carp is returned to the water quickly and safely to give other anglers the rush of catching these fish. Holding the carp correctly also reduces the chance of damaging any fins on the fish, which will have a massive effect. If fins are damaged, the fish may have issues swimming to find food, reproducing, feeding issues and many more. Also, if the fish is dropped on debris, this can damage scales, resulting in infections and even the death of the fish.

Carp are also covered in a layer of protective slime that acts as part of their immune system. Extreme care needs to be taken not to wash this layer off when handling the fish. These fish are also cold blooded creatures and can react strongly when touched by our warm hands and wrists. Due to this, care must be taken when handling the fish and measures can be taken to reduce the discomfort for the fish.

I'm sure you can now see why its so important to handle carp correct, and I'll now get into how to handle carp properly with a step by step guide.

How to Hold Carp – Step by Step
1. Slide Hands Under Carp

1. The first step to hold a carp properly is to kneel down as close and as low to the fish as possible.

2. You should then slide your hands under the body of the fish. The hand closest to the head of the fish should slide in from the head towards the gills. Be very careful with the eye on the underside of the fish.

3. You should then grasp either side of the front pectoral fin, as you can see in the picture above.

4. The hand closest to the tail should slide under towards the anal fin where you should grasp either side. Be very careful not to lift any scales when doing this.

2. Turning Carp Over

1. Once your hands are slid under and in these positions on either side of the fish, you can turn the fish over into a lifting position.

2. By slowly tilting your hands and using your forearms, you should tilt the fish around, so it is upright.

3. Make sure and keep the fish as close to the mat as possible in case the fish starts to struggle.

4. Once the fish is in this position, you can either stay kneeling or get into a squat position. This is entirely personal preference, but staying in the kneeling position should be the easiest.

3. Lifting the Carp

1. Once the fish is turned over and secured tightly, you can lift it from the mat. Once again though, you don't want to remove the fish too far from the mat so avoid standing up with your fish.
2. Hold the fish close to your body for more support.
3. You can even keep your elbows on your knees if the fish is heavy so you can hold it for a little longer.

4. Holding the Carp for a Photo

1. Keep a good grip on the fins and use your hands to keep the fish balanced and secured.
2. You can even keep your elbows on your knees if the fish is heavy, so you can hold it for a little longer.

Dealing with Struggling Carp

The carp may still be active when on the banks and begin the wriggle and flip in many cases. If this is the case, you need to take some steps to ensure the carp does not injure itself. If this starts to happen through the lift, tilt the fish back onto your forearms and carefully lower it back down onto the wet unhooking mat.

If it continues to struggle, you can place a hand over its eye to try to calm it down. If this is the case, you should also pour some water from the lake over the fish to keep it calm and cool. This should be all the information you need to learn how to handle carp correctly. The process is simple but will take a bit of practice at the start.

Conclusion

Go and Catch Some Carp

We're sure you should now be armed with plenty of info to improve your carp fishing game and get you into some nice fish over your subsequent sessions. You should have gained a wealth of information into:

- How to identify the fish you are most likely to come across on your sessions and a bit about their background.
- How carp behave under the water's surface and how this relates to your fishing approach.
- How to choose the correct carp fishing tackle and how each piece is commonly used.
- How to learn carp fishing "watercraft" to perfect your carp locating skills so you can be sure you're fishing effective swims to give yourself the best chance of success.
- The best baits to choose, how to utilise them effectively and which baits you should be choosing for specific carp fishing rigs and approaches.
- The best rigs for carp fishing, how to use them and the pros and cons of each.
- How to properly look after carp once they are on the banks and the steps to taking the perfect picture while avoiding injury to the fish.

Now what are you waiting for? Get yourself on the banks and catch some fish!

We hope you have enjoyed this book. If you have any feedback or anything you would like to see added to this book, you can send an email to:

Drew@bestofangling.com

Also, if you would like to receive a free PDF eBook copy of any updated new editions of this book, drop us an email, and you will receive a copy straight to your email on release.

Printed in Great Britain
by Amazon

81695311R00086